KT-375-150

POETRY

HORIZONS

Volume 1

Edited by
Richard Andrews
and
Ian Bentley

Bell & Hyman

Published in 1987 by
Bell & Hyman
An imprint of Unwin Hyman Limited
Denmark House
37–39 Queen Elizabeth Street
London SE1 2QB

Selection and notes © Richard Andrews and
Ian Bentley 1987
The copyright of each poem remains the
property of the author

All rights reserved. No part of this publication
may be reproduced, stored in a retrieval
system, or transmitted in any form or by any
means, electronic, mechanical, photocopying,
recording or otherwise, without the prior
permission of Bell & Hyman

British Library Cataloguing in Publication Data
Poetry horizons.
   1. English poetry
   I. Andrews, Richard   II. Bentley, Ian
   821'.008'09282   PR1175

   ISBN 0–7135–2679–3 v.1
   ISBN 0–7135–2680–7 v.2

Designed by Geoffrey Wadsley
Typeset by Latimer Trend & Company Ltd,
Plymouth
Printed in Great Britain by
R. J. Acford Ltd, Chichester

Contents

Introduction: to the teacher

How we perceive poetry & its role in English

It might be argued that, although it is often disliked by pupils and shunned by teachers, poetry is the single most important element in the teaching of English. A careful study of poetry involves all a student's analytical skills and demands a focusing of the critical sense on a text of an easily assimilable length. The length of all the poems we have selected will enable students to see a literary work as an artistic and emotional whole. Too often in 'English', works are used as if they were a collection of fragments to be quarried for various purposes: a study of character or theme, for example, or simply as a basis for students' personal writing. There is a value in these approaches but only with poetry can a fourth or fifth year student learn to grasp a work of art in its entirety, as a cogent and coherent whole. In using poetry in the classroom, the necessity for silent reading, performed reading and private thought provides an almost ideal situation for group or class discussion of what will then be shared experience.

The study of poetry encourages students to be aware of language and its extraordinary power. Poetry incorporates a vast range of experience and expression, from polemic to the most delicate shades of meaning and sugges- tion. A study of poetry involves the awareness of rhythm, rhyme, assonance, alliteration, simile, metaphor—in short, all the ways we can manipulate language to suit our purposes and express ourselves lucidly and concisely rather than allowing ourselves to be manipulated by language in its everyday form.

We believe that a study of poetry, which necessitates an active involvement with the text, will enhance students' critical skills, broaden their awareness of form and language usage, and thus enable them to perceive themselves and others more clearly and to form their ideas about themselves and their relationships with the world more securely.

The structure of the anthology

This first book divides into five sections: Observing, Telling, Transforming, Reflecting and Childhood. The structure embodies a suggested teaching ap- proach as well as providing a theory of poetic composition which moves from the raw material of the senses ('Observing'), through narrative poetry of various kinds (not only ballads) to the transformational powers of poetic language (the way that, for example, metaphor conveys feeling) and finally to the reflective mode (the traditional mode of much world poetry). The Childhood section is provided as an example of how poems can be grouped around a theme. These poems contain the four previous modes of poetic language (as do many others in the book) and form a fitting conclusion to this, the first of two anthologies for students studying English and English Literature for the General Certificate of Secondary Education.

You may wish to follow the structure outlined here, in which case it is probably best to approach the five sections one by one at intervals through the school year. On the other hand, you might prefer to adapt the poems and other resources offered by this book to your own programme and teaching style.

What we have offered here, in addition to an anthology that is structured according to kinds of poetic language rather than to 'themes', are 'key' poems in each section which might form the focus of a student's written work; notes on each poem to explain allusions and references, to draw attention to important points and to suggest activities arising from the poems; appendices with ideas for developing work in students' coursework folders, a glossary specifically written for the poems in the selection and an index suggesting cross-referencing by theme.

General suggestions for work with poems

We feel it is important in the fourth year to maintain the momentum of interest in poetry generated in the first three years of secondary English, and to keep the poems accessible and engaging. Not all work arising from—or preceding—the reading of poems need be narrowly analytical.

We offer here some suggestions for work with poems that can be used with any of the poems in this collection, and indeed any others you may wish to use.

Enacting

1   Rehearsed readings: preparing to read a poem aloud will entail a close analysis of its tone, rhythm and intention. Poems can be memorised, taped, etc.
2   Displays: including illustrations.
3   Making an anthology: as a project, this can move beyond the compilation of a written or printed anthology to displays, recordings and presentations.
4   Choral readings: ballads, poems with refrains and poems using more than one 'voice' are particularly suitable.
5   Parody and imitation: writing in the style or form of a particular poem.
6   Writing: on similar themes *before* a poem is read helps prepare the ground.
7   Listening: to poets themselves, and to readings on tape.
8   Writing courses: with professional poets or with you, the teacher.
9   Dramatisation: many poems lend themselves to direct dramatisation or provide themes, situations and language that can form the basis of improvisation and other types of dramatic development.

Reflection and discussion

1   First impressions: students listen to two or three readings of a poem, or read it silently; then jot their first impressions as a basis for further discussion in small groups; then with the class as a whole.
2   Small group discussion: formally at first, based on statements about the poem; then simply around an unseen poem (with or without tape recorder).
3   Cloze: although apparently artificial, this can be a useful technique for

focusing attention upon particular elements in a poem.

4 Sequencing: can be done by the line, or by the stanza, and offers a practical approach to the structure and development of a poem.

5 Making a title: give an untitled poem, and ask students to compose a title. This can be discussed, then compared with the actual title of the poem.

6 Writing it out as prose: what is lost?

7 Making up questions: students can devise a list of questions, both factual and analytical, for other groups. This could be linked with the anthology.

List of Poems

* Key poem

Section 1: Observing

Section 2: Telling

Section 3: Transforming

Section 4: Reflecting

Section 5: Childhood

List of Illustrations

The Snack Bar, 1930, by Edward Burra, Tate Gallery, London; p8

Extract page from *Brouillard au Pont du Tolbiac* by Leo Melet/Tardi, published in 1982 by Casterman, Paris; p36

Study for Portrait, 1971, by Francis Bacon, Private Collection, London; p72

A Bigger Splash, 1967, by David Hockney, Tate Gallery, London; p90

Hilda, Unity and Dolls, 1937, by Sir Stanley Spencer, Leeds City Art Gallery, reproduced by consent of the Trustees of the Artist's Estate, London; p116

Section 1
Observing

The Snack Bar
Edward Burra

*O*bservation is important in poetry. A poet likes to keep his eyes open—and his ears. And, indeed, he wants to keep all his senses sharp and active, since poetry reflects the whole of human experience, including the most physical. On the other hand, the actual physical observation is not everything. A poet must have imagination, and part of his job is to be able to visualise, to see with his inward eye, things that he may not himself have seen, or at least not exactly as he wants to imagine them. He can describe things in his poetry either from direct observation or from imagination, and—strange as it may seem—the reader of the poem may not be able to tell the difference. But, of course, the imagination itself has to work on the poet's stored-up memories of a myriad impressions, images, pictures, which come from experience.

As far as observation is concerned, writers who live in large cities and use urban material develop—instinctively!—a very quick, unstudied, unprying, oblique, yet intense and unforgetful way of looking at people and things: it's like using a very good silent automatic camera disguised as a pair of eyes. To look too long at anyone is dangerous (in Glasgow at any rate—I don't know about other places), and so the rapid flickering scan is characteristic of the urban poet. The many minute impressions are a shorthand which he can expand later within the (slightly!) less nervous world of the poem.

EDWIN MORGAN

Glasgow 5 March 1971

With a ragged diamond
of shattered plate-glass
a young man and his girl
are falling backwards into a shop-window.
The young man's face
is bristling with fragments of glass
and the girl's leg has caught
on the broken window
and spurts arterial blood
over her wet-look white coat.   *10*
Their arms are starfished out
braced for impact,
their faces show surprise, shock,
and the beginning of pain.
The two youths who have pushed them
are about to complete the operation
reaching into the window
to loot what they can smartly.
Their faces show no expression.
It is a sharp clear night   *20*
in Sauchiehall Street.
In the background two drivers
Keep their eyes on the road.

Edwin Morgan

Glasgow 5 March 1971

Quickly the magistrate
has ducked to the left.
The knife is just hitting the wall
a few inches away. Already the police
have their hands on the man in the dock
whose right arm is still stretched out
where the weapon left it. One feature
of this picture of the Central Police Court
is the striking absence of consternation.

Edwin Morgan

10

Chicago May 1971

The elegant vice-presidential office of U.S. Steel
is the scene of a small ceremony.
A man has placed a miniature coffin
on the vice-president's couch, and in the coffin
you can see frog, perch, crawfish, dead.
They have swallowed the laborious effluent
of U.S. Steel in Lake Michigan.
The man is poised ready to run,
wrinkling his nose as he pours from a held-out bottle
a dark brown viscous Michigan sludge
over the vice-president's white rug. This is
the eco-man. On the table his card,
The fox.

Edwin Morgan

In The Huon Valley

Propped boughs are heavy with apples,
Springtime quite forgotten.
Pears ripen yellow. The wasp
Knows where windfalls lie rotten.

Juices grow rich with sun.
These autumn days are still:
The glassy river reflects
Elm-gold up the hill,

And big white plumes of rushes.
Life is full of returns;   *10*
It isn't true that one never
Profits, never learns:

Something is gathered in,
Worth the lifting and stacking;
Apples roll through the graders,
The sheds are noisy with packing.

James McAuley

11

Tinker's Wife

I saw her amid the dunghill debris
Looking for things
Such as an old pair of shoes or gaiters.
She was a young woman,
A tinker's wife.
Her face had streaks of care
Like wires across it,
But she was supple
As a young goat
On a windy hill.   *10*

She searched on the dunghill debris,
Tripping gingerly
Over tin canisters
And sharp-broken
Dinner plates.

Patrick Kavanagh

New Year's morning

the children come searching
among the scattered red of the road
for unexploded crackers,
turning over the charred heaps
and eagerly picking up one or two;

the night's dews have made tham damp,
they no longer sound sharply,
but even a flash and a pop
is an artistic success,
an event of power.   *10*

their small faces smile a celebration

as echoes rock the neighbourhood,
machine-gun into the new year.

Lee Tzu Pheng

Digging

Between my finger and my thumb
The squat pen rests; snug as a gun.

Under my window, a clean rasping sound
When the spade sinks into gravelly ground:
My father, digging. I look down

Till his straining rump among the flowerbeds
Bends low, comes up twenty years away
Stooping in rhythm through potato drills
Where he was digging.

The coarse boot nestled on the lug, the shaft   *10*
Against the inside knee was levered firmly.
He rooted out tall tops, buried the bright edge deep
To scatter new potatoes that we picked
Loving their cool hardness in our hands.

By God, the old man could handle a spade.
Just like his old man.

My grandfather cut more turf in a day
Than any other man on Toner's bog.
Once I carried him milk in a bottle
Corked sloppily with paper. He straightened up   *20*
To drink it, then fell to right away
Nicking and slicing neatly, heaving sods
Over his shoulder, going down and down
For the good turf. Digging.

The cold smell of potato mould, the squelch and slap
Of soggy peat, the curt cuts of an edge
Through living roots awaken in my head.
But I've no spade to follow men like them.

Between my finger and my thumb
The squat pen rests.   *30*
I'll dig with it.

Seamus Heaney

13

The French Master

Everyone in class two at the Grammar School
had heard of Walter Bird, known as Wazo.
They said he'd behead each dullard and fool
or, instead, carve off a tail for fun.

Wazo's cane buzzed like a bee in the air.
Quietly, quietly, in the desks of Form III
sneaky Wazo tweaked our ears and our hair.
Walter Wazo, public enemy No. 1.

Five feet tall, he married sweet Doreen Wall
and combmarks his vaselined hair;   *10*
his hands still fluttering ridiculously small,
His eyes the colour of a poison bottle.

Who'd think he'd falter poor love-sick Walter
As bored he read out Lettres de Mon Moulin;
His mouth had begun to soften and alter,
And Class IV ribbed him as only boys can.

Perhaps through kissing his wife to a moan
had alone changed the shape of his lips,
till the habit of her mouth became his own;
No more Walter Wazo, Public Enemy No. 1.   *20*

'Boy' he'd whine, 'yes, please decline the verb to hate,'
In tones dulcet and mild as a girl's,
'Sorry Sir, can't Sir, must go to the lav,'
Whilst Wazo stared out of this world.

Till one day in May Wazo buzzed like a bee,
And stung twice many a warm, inky hand;
he stormed through the form, a catastrophe
returned to this world, No. 1.

Alas, alas, to the VIth Form's disgrace
nobody could quote Villon to that villain.   *30*
Again the nasty old mouth zipped on his face,
And not a weak-bladdered boy in the class.

Was Doreen being kissed by a Mr Anon?
Years later I purred, 'Your dear wife, Mr Bird?'
Teeth bared, how he glared before stamping on;
And suddenly I felt sorry for the bastard.

Dannie Abse

The Artist

Mr T.
        bareheaded
                in a soiled undershirt
his hair standing out
        on all sides
                stood on his toes
heels together
        arms gracefully
                for the moment
curled above his head.   *10*
        Then he whirled about
                bounded
into the air
        and with an entrechat
                perfectly achieved
completed the figure.
        My mother
                taken by surprise
where she sat
        in her invalid's chair
                was left speechless.   *20*
Bravo! she cried at last
        and clapped her hands.
                The man's wife
came from the kitchen:
        What goes on here? she said.
                But the show was over.

William Carlos Williams

In The Snack-Bar

A cup capsizes along the formica,
slithering with a dull clatter.
A few heads turn in the crowded evening snack-bar.
An old man is trying to get to his feet
from the low round stool fixed to the floor.
Slowly he levers himself up, his hands have no power.
He is up as far as he can get. The dismal hump
looming over him forces his head down.
He stands in his stained beltless gaberdine
like a monstrous animal caught in a tent   10
in some story. He sways slightly,
the face not seen, bent down
in shadow under his cap.
Even on his feet he is staring at the floor
or would be, if he could see.
I notice now his stick, once painted white
but scuffed and muddy, hanging from his right arm.
Long blind, hunchback born, half paralysed
he stands
fumbling with the stick   20
and speaks:
'I want—to go to the—toilet.'

It is down two flights of stairs, but we go.
I take his arm. 'Give me—your arm—it's better,' he says.
Inch by inch we drift towards the stairs.
A few yards of floor are like a landscape
to be negotiated, in the slow setting out
time has almost stopped. I concentrate
my life to his: crunch of spilt sugar
slidy puddle from the night's umbrellas,   30
table edges, people's feet,
hiss of the coffee-machine, voices and laughter,
smell of a cigar, hamburgers, wet coats steaming,
and the slow dangerous inches to the stairs.
I put his right hand on the rail
and take his stick. He clings to me. The stick
is in his left hand, probing the treads.
I guide his arm and tell him the steps.
And slowly we go down. And slowly we go down.

White tiles and mirrors at last. He shambles   40
uncouth into the clinical gleam.
I set him in position, stand behind him
and wait with his stick.
His brooding reflection darkens the mirror
but the trickle of his water is thin and slow,
an old man's apology for living.
Painful ages to close his trousers and coat—
I do up the last buttons for him.
He asks doubtfully, 'Can I—wash my hands?'
I fill the basin, clasp his soft fingers round the soap.   50
He washes feebly, patiently. There is no towel.
I press the pedal of the drier, draw his hands
gently into the roar of the hot air.
But he cannot rub them together,
drags out a handkerchief to finish.
He is glad to leave the contraption, and face the stairs.
He climbs, and steadily enough.
He climbs, we climb. He climbs
with many pauses but with that one
persisting patience of the undefeated   60
which is the nature of man when all is said.
And slowly we go up. And slowly we go up.
The faltering, unfaltering steps
take him at last to the door
across that endless, yet not endless waste of floor.
I watch him helped on a bus. It shudders off in the rain.
The conductor bends to hear where he wants to go.
Wherever he could go it would be dark
and yet he must trust men.
Without embarrassment or shame   70
he must annouce his most pitiful needs
in a public place. No one sees his face.
Does he know how frightening he is in his strangeness
under his mountainous coat, his hands like wet leaves
stuck to the half-white stick?
His life depends on many who would evade him.
But he cannot reckon up the chances,
having one thing to do,
to haul his blind hump through these rains of August.
Dear Christ, to be born for this!

Edwin Morgan

Exposure

Our brains ache, in the merciless iced east winds that knive us . . .
Wearied we keep awake because the night is silent . . .
Low, drooping flares confuse our memory of the salient . . .
Worried by silence, sentries whisper, curious, nervous,
       But nothing happens.

Watching, we hear the mad gusts tugging on the wire,
Like twitching agonies of men among its brambles.
Northward, incessantly, the flickering gunnery rumbles,
Far off, like a dull rumour of some other war.
       What are we doing here?   *10*

The poignant misery of dawn begins to grow . . .
We only know war lasts, rain soaks, and clouds sag stormy.
Dawn massing in the east her melancholy army
Attacks once more in ranks on shivering ranks of gray,
       But nothing happens.

Sudden successive flights of bullets streak the silence.
Less deadly than the air that shudders black with snow,
With sidelong flowing flakes that flock, pause, and renew,
We watch them wandering up and down the wind's nonchalance,
       But nothing happens.   *20*

Pale flakes with fingering stealth come feeling for our faces—
We cringe in holes, back on forgotten dreams, and stare,
    snow-dazed,
Deep into grassier ditches. So we drowse, sun-dozed,
Littered with blossoms trickling where the blackbird fusses.
       Is it that we are dying?

Slowly our ghosts drag home: glimpsing the sunk fires, glozed
With crusted dark-red jewels; crickets jingle there;
For hours the innocent mice rejoice: the house is theirs;
Shutters and doors, all closed: on us the doors are closed,—
       We turn back to our dying.   *30*

Since we believe not otherwise can kind fires burn;
Nor ever suns smile true on child, or field, or fruit.
For God's invincible spring our love is made afraid;
Therefore, not loath, we lie out here; therefore were born.
        For love of God seems dying.

Tonight, His frost will fasten on this mud and us,
Shrivelling many hands, puckering foreheads crisp.
The burying-party, picks and shovels in their shaking grasp,
Pause over half-known faces. All their eyes are ice,
        But nothing happens.

Wilfred Owen

Digging

To-day I think
Only with scents,—scents dead leaves yield,
And bracken, and wild carrot's seed,
And the square mustard field;

Odours that rise
When the spade wounds the root of tree,
Rose, currant, raspberry, or goutweed,
Rhubarb or celery;

The smoke's smell, too,
Flowing from where a bonfire burns   *10*
The dead, the waste, the dangerous,
And all to sweetness turns.

It is enough
To smell, to crumble the dark earth,
While the robin sings over again
Sad songs of Autumn mirth.

Edward Thomas

19

A March Calf

Right from the start he is dressed in his best—his blacks and his
    whites.
Little Fauntleroy—quiffed and glossy,
A Sunday suit, a wedding natty get-up,
Standing in dunged straw.

Under cobwebby beams, near the mud wall,
Half of him legs,
Shining-eyed, requiring nothing more
But that mother's milk come back often.

Everything else is in order, just as it is.
Let the summer skies hold off, for the moment.   *10*
That is just as he wants it.
A little at a time, of each new thing, is best.

Too much and too sudden is too frightening—
When I block the light, a bulk from space,
To let him in to his mother for a suck,
He bolts a yard or two, then freezes,

Staring from every hair in all directions,
Ready for the worst, shut up in his hopeful religion,
A little syllogism
With a wet blue-reddish muzzle, for God's thumb.   *20*

You see all his hopes bustling
As he reaches between the worn rails towards
The topheavy oven of his mother.
He trembles to grow, stretching his curl-tip tongue—

What did cattle ever find here
To make this dear little fellow
So eager to prepare himself?
He is already in the race, and quivering to win—

His new purpled eyeball swivel-jerks
In the elbowing push of his plans.   *30*
Hungry people are getting hungrier,
Butchers developing expertise and markets,

20

But he just wobbles his tail—and glistens
Within his dapper profile
Unaware of how his whole lineage
Has been tied up.

He shivers for feel of the world licking his side.
He is like an ember—one glow
Of lighting himself up
With the fuel of himself, breathing and brightening.   *40*

Soon he'll plunge out, to scatter his seething joy,
To be present at the grass,
To be free on the surface of such a wideness,
To find himself himself. To stand. To moo.

Ted Hughes

Dedicatory Poem

This morning from a dewy motorway
I saw the new camp for the internees:
a bomb had left a crater of fresh clay
in the roadside, and over in the trees

machine-gun posts defined a real stockade.
There was that white mist you get on a low ground
and it was déjà-vu, some film made
of Stalag 17, a bad dream with no sound.

Is there a life before death? That's chalked up
on a wall downtown. Competence with pain,   *10*
coherent miseries, a bite and sup,
we hug our little destiny again.

Seamus Heaney

21

Snake

A snake came to my water-trough
On a hot, hot day, and I in pyjamas for the heat,
To drink there.

In the deep, strange-scented shade of the great dark carob-tree
I came down the steps with my pitcher
And must wait, must stand and wait, for there he was at the trough
    before me.

He reached down from a fissure in the earth-wall in the gloom
And trailed his yellow-brown slackness soft-bellied down, over the
    edge of the stone trough
And rested his throat upon the stone bottom,
And where the water had dripped from the tap, in a small
    clearness,   *10*
He sipped with his straight mouth,
Softly drank through his straight gums, into his slack long body,
Silently.

Someone was before me at my water-trough,
And I, like a second comer, waiting.

He lifted his head from his drinking, as cattle do,
And looked at me vaguely, as drinking cattle do,
And flickered his two-forked tongue from his lips, and mused a
    moment,
And stooped and drank a little more,
Being earth-brown, earth-golden from the burning bowels of the
    earth   *20*
On the day of Sicilian July, with Etna smoking.
The voice of my education said to me
He must be killed,
For in Sicily the black, black snakes are innocent, the gold are
    venomous.

And voices in me said, If you were a man
You would take a stick and break him now, and finish him off.

But must I confess how I liked him,
How glad I was he had come like a guest in quiet, to drink at my
    water-trough
And depart peaceful, pacified, and thankless,
Into the burning bowels of this earth?   *30*

Was it cowardice, that I dared not kill him?
Was it perversity, that I longed to talk to him?
Was it humility, to feel so honoured?
I felt so honoured.

And yet those voices:
If you were not afraid, you would kill him!

And truly I was afraid, I was most afraid,
But even so, honoured still more
That he should seek my hospitality
From out the dark door of the secret earth.   *40*

He drank enough
And lifted his head, dreamily, as one who has drunken,
And flickered his tongue like a forked night on the air, so black,
Seeming to lick his lips,
And looked around like a god, unseeing, into the air,
And slowly turned his head,
And slowly, very slowly, as if thrice adream,
Proceeded to draw his slow length curving round
And climb again the broken bank of my wall-face.

And as he put his head into that dreadful hole,   *50*
And as he slowly drew up, snake-easing his shoulders, and entered
    farther,
A sort of horror, a sort of protest against his withdrawing into that
    horrid black hole,
Deliberately going into the blackness, and slowly drawing himself
    after,
Overcame me now his back was turned.

I looked round, I put down my pitcher,
I picked up a clumsy log
And threw it at the water-trough with a clatter.

I think it did not hit him,
But suddenly that part of him that was left behind convulsed in
        undignified haste,
Writhed like lightning, and was gone   60
Into the black hole, the earth-lipped fissure in the wall-front,
At which, in the intense still noon, I stared with fascination.

And immediately I regretted it.
I thought how paltry, how vulgar, what a mean act!
I despised myself and the voices of my accursed human education.

And I thought of the albatross,
And I wished he would come back, my snake.

For he seemed to me again like a king,
Like a king in exile, uncrowned in the underworld,
Now due to be crowned again.   70

And so, I missed my chance with one of the lords
Of life.
And I have something to expiate;
A pettiness.

D. H. Lawrence

Praise Of A Collie

She was a small dog, neat and fluid—
Even her conversation was tiny:
She greeted you with *bow*, never *bow-wow*.

Her sons stood monumentally over her
But did what she told them. Each grew grizzled
Till it seemed he was his own mother's grandfather.

Once, gathering sheep on a showery day,
I remarked how dry she was. Pollochan said, 'Ah,
It would take a very accurate drop to hit Lassie.'

And her tact—and tactics! When the sheep bolted   10
In an unforeseen direction, over the skyline
Came—who but Lassie, and not even panting.

She sailed in the dinghy like a proper sea-dog.
Where's a burn?—she's first on the other side.
She flowed through fences like a piece of black wind.

But suddenly she was old and sick and crippled . . .
I grieved for Pollochan when he took her a stroll
And put his gun to the back of her head.

Norman MacCaig

Late Night Walk Down Terry Street

A policeman on a low-powered motorcycle stops.
His radio crackles, his helmet yellows.

Empty buses heading for the depot
Rush past the open end of Terry Street.

In their light, a man with a bike walking home,
Too drunk to ride it, turns into Terry Street.

Taxis swerve down Terry Street's shortcut,
Down uneven halls of Street Lighting Department yellow.

Into which now comes the man with the bike,
Struggling to keep on his legs.   *10*

The policeman waits under a gone-out streetlamp.
He stops the drunk, they talk, they laugh together.

I pass them then, beside dark, quiet houses,
In others mumbling sounds of entertainment;

Cathode-glows through curtains, faint latest tunes;
Creaking of bedsprings, lights going out.

Douglas Dunn

Nature

We have neither Summer nor Winter,
Neither Autumn nor Spring.

We have instead the days
When gold sun shines on the lush green canefields—
Magnificently.

The days when the rain beats like bullets on the roofs
And there is no sound but the swish of water in the gullies
And trees struggling in the high Jamaica winds.

Also there are the days when the leaves fade from off guango trees
And the reaped canefields lie bare and fallow in the sun.   *10*

But best of all there are the days when the mango and the logwood
    blossom.

When the bushes are full of the sound of bees and the scent of
    honey,
When the tall grass sways and shivers to the slightest breath of air,

When the buttercups have paved the earth with yellow stars,
And beauty comes suddenly and the rains have gone.

H. D. Carberry

Camping Provençal

Camping Provençal. Notices: (1)
Tourists may only settle in the camp,
after if having checked in at the office
they know their places. (2) The campers' dresses
must be correct in camp. (3) Please no noise
between the 22 and seven-o-clock.
(4) In the camp, parents must watch across
their children. (5) Take care of the plantations,
don't set up nails nor pour dish-water on
the trees. (6) Fire-woods are forbidden. (7)   *10*
Linen must dry discreetly. (8) Detritus,
put this into the dustbins. (9) Showers-bath,
wash-house and W.C. must be kept clean.
Water is quite uncommon in Provence.
(10) Management is NOT responsible
for thefts. (11) Speed don't exceed 5.
(12) *That* box is reserved alone for throw
sanitary-towels and periodicals.
(13) These rules must be respected under
penalty of your time expiring here.   *20*

Peter Reading

Notes and activities

How to use the notes and activities
*Term included in the Glossary

The *Questions to discuss* are for oral work either in class or in smaller groups.

The sections of notes in italics suggest possible writing activities arising from each poem.

The key poems between double rules have more detailed notes and might form the focus of your coursework.

Glasgow 5 March 1971   ('With a ragged diamond')
Glasgow 5 March 1971   ('Quickly the magistrate')
Chicago May 1971   *Edwin Morgan*
In the second poem 'Sauchiehall Street' is one of the main streets in the centre of Glasgow. 'Sauchiehall' is pronounced 'Sekkiehall'. In the third poem, Chicago is a major American city on the shores of Lake Michigan.

Question to discuss
Edwin Morgan calls these 'Instamatic Poems' or 'takes'. Can you work out why?

Try your own 'Instamatic Poems'. Remember you have to catch a single moment.

In The Huon Valley   *James McAuley*
The Huon Valley is just west of Hobart in Tasmania, the island off the southern tip of Australia. It is one of the southernmost parts of the cultivated world, but is only as far from the equator as Paris. Autumn is taking place there when it is springtime in the Northern hemisphere.

Questions for discussion
Here is a series of statements about the poem. Discuss them in small groups, and then decide which three are the most important and rank them in order:
1   The overall impression is one of movement and life.
2   The key line in the poem is "Life is full of returns".
3   "glassy" in line 7 suggests the river is flat and hard.
4   "Propped" in the first line is used to give the sense of old trees in need of support.
5   There is no rhyming in the poem.

6 "Graders" in line 15 are machines, not people.
7 The last line is a good ending.
8 The "returns" in line 10 refers to the profits made by the farmers.
9 The poem is about apples.
10 The poem is about autumn.
Then report to the class as a whole.

Tinker's Wife   *Patrick Kavanagh*
'tinker': a wandering craftsman who mends pots and pans
'gaiters': leather coverings for the ankle and lower leg

Questions to discuss
This poem is built around contrasts. What are they?
Does Kavanagh admire her or not? What does the simile* on line 7 suggest
about her, as well as her suppleness?

New Year's Morning   *Lee Tzu Pheng*
Not January 1st, but Chinese New Year which usually falls in February and is
celebrated with fireworks

Questions to discuss
What is the effect of the image in the last line, where echoes 'machine-gun
into the new year'? What aspect of machine-gunning is intended, do you
think?

Digging   *Seamus Heaney*
'potato drills': the lines in which potatoes are planted
'lug': the part of the spade at the top of the blade

Questions to discuss ·
What does the image 'snug as a gun' suggest about the pen?
How is writing like digging in the poem?
Do you think the poem is about:
   —digging
   —family tradition
   —writing
   —all three of these things?
*Compare this poem with the one by Edward Thomas, also called 'Digging'.
You could start by drawing up a simple chart, like this one which has been
started for you:*

Similarities	*Differences*	
	Thomas	*Heaney*
Use of senses, esp. smell	Poet digging	Observing father dig

*You could use this as the starting point for a longer piece of writing for a
coursework folder.*
*Alternatively, you could compare two poems by Seamus Heaney, this one
and 'Dedicatory Poem' on page 21.*

30

The French Master   *Dannie Abse*

'Oiseau' is the French for bird, hence *Wazo*.
Lettres de Mon Moulin is by the 19th century writer, Alphonse Daudet.
Villon is a 15th century French poet.

Questions for writing
(*either before or after discussion*)
1   What effect does marrying Doreen Wall have on Walter Bird as a teacher?
2   Why is Wazo described as 'buzzing' in the seventh stanza? What is his teaching like after this?
3   How many stages are there in the depiction of the French master?
4   Why does the poet feel sorry for him in the last line?
5   Who do you think the 'I' of the poem is?

The Artist   *William Carlos Williams*

'entrechat': a leap in which the dancer beats his or her heels together
'figure': movement

Questions to discuss
Why do you think this poem is called 'The Artist'? Why is the poet concerned to note that his mother sat 'in her invalid's chair'? What does the entrance of the third person, the man's wife, add to the poem?

If you have access to a space for drama, you could use this poem as a starting point for a group of three to explore the relationship between the three characters. What might happen next? What tensions might there be between the three? What might have happened before the event?

In The Snack-Bar   *Edwin Morgan*

Before reading this poem carefully, you might like to write about a person who is less fortunate than yourself. You can do this either as a poem or a prose-piece, but you should take the writing further than the 'noting/observing' stage. It can be based on actual observation or imagined/remembered observation, or a combination of the two. Whichever approach you take, you should focus on *details* of the person, and of his or her setting* too,
This piece of writing may form part of your English coursework folder. If you can't think of a subject, use one of these:
       'The tramp'
       'The outcast'

Now re-read Edwin Morgan's poem more slowly. How different is 'In the Snack Bar' from your account?

31

Questions for discussion
(in pairs, small groups or the whole class)

1 'like a monstrous animal caught in a tent' (l.10)
   'A few yards of floor are like a landscape
   to be negotiated . . .' (ll.26–27)
   '. . . his hands like wet leaves
   stuck to the half-white stick?' (ll.74–75)
   What does each image* tell us about Morgan's feelings about the old
   man?
2 What observation is there in the poem that communicates the
   poets's attitude to the old man?
3 What *is* the poet's attitude to the old man? Does it change during the
   poem?
4 Find the details about the old man noticed by the poet. What do they
   tell us about the old man?
5 This poem *tells a story* as well as being a closely observed account of
   an old man. In what way is the poem story-like?

Now that you have read and re-read the poem, would you change your
initial piece of writing in any way?

Exposure   *Wilfred Owen*

This poem was written from the trenches during the First World War.

'salient': prominent, most important
'melancholy': miserable, gloomy
'glozed': it usually means to flatter, but that can't be its meaning here. What do
you think Owen is intending?
'loath': the same as 'loth', unwilling, reluctant

Questions to discuss

The first four stanzas are concerned with the situation in the trenches. But
what happens in the fifth? What do you think the 'forgotten dreams' are?
Where are the 'grassier ditches'? The 'blossoms trickling' are probably
suggested by the snow in stanza 4, but *where* are they?

*When you have read the poem several times, focus your group discussions on
stanzas 6 and 7, the most difficult part of the poem. See if your group can
work out what Owen intends in these stanzas, and then report back to the rest
of the class.*
*Then, as an entire class, puzzle out the last stanza: something is happening,
and yet 'nothing happens'. What is the meaning and effect of that repeated
phrase, 'But nothing happens'.*

Digging   *Edward Thomas*

'goutweed': a weed growing in ditches, streams or drains
'mirth': as used here, a 'poetic' or old-fashioned word for rejoicing

Questions to discuss
Is the poem a celebration (i.e. a happy poem) or not?
This poem is built around contrasts. What are they?

This poem could form a key part of writing on the senses. Clearly the principal sense here is that of smell—the olfactory sense—but which poems in this section would you choose to write about if you were asked to write on all the senses?

  sight—visual
  hearing—aural
  touch—sensual
  taste—gustatory

Which of these five senses is used most in the observations contained in the poems in this section? Do you think this is a fair representation of most people's experience?

A March Calf   *Ted Hughes*

'Little (Lord) Fauntleroy': a character in literature; a young boy always beautifully dressed in velvet and lace
'natty': neat and smart
'syllogism': a logical argument, like $A + B = C$

Questions to discuss
Work through the poem in detail and note the phrases which aren't straight description of the calf, but which borrow from human experience. An example is the image of the 'Sunday suit' in the first stanza. What does each image suggest about the calf?

What do you notice about the last stanza? Why do you think Hughes wrote it in this way?

Dedicatory Poem   *Seamus Heaney*

This poem is so-called because it was used by Heaney to dedicate his third volume of poetry, *Wintering Out*, to his Belfast friends, David Hammond and Michael Longley.
'internees': people interned or imprisoned for political reasons
'déjà-vu': already seen—you feel as though you've seen this before

Questions to discuss
The graffiti 'Is there a life before death?' is a version of what more usual question? What do you think he means by 'coherent miseries'? What is the suggestion of the last line?

This poem describes a scene in Ulster, but it also conveys a political message. How does it do that, without saying anything explicitly? You might like to try writing a poem about an issue or event or a person that you have strong feeling about. Try, as Heaney has done, to keep your eye on the subject and to convey your message through detail, rather than spelling it out.*

Snake   *D. H. Lawrence*

'carob tree': also known as the 'locust tree' and found in the Mediterranean countries

'Sicilian': Sicily is an island off the southernmost coast of Italy, and 'Etna' is its volcanic mountain

'expiate': to pay for or make up for a crime or wrongdoing

Questions to discuss

Does the writer admire or hate the snake? How can you tell?

When he thinks 'of the albatross' towards the end, he is thinking of the famous poem by Coleridge, *The Ancient Mariner*, in which a sailor shoots an albatross and lives to regret it. What is this writer's feeling at the end of the poem?

Take a photocopy of the poem and cut it into its sections or paragraphs. Put aside the original copy, and see if you can re-construct the poem with a friend. When you have finished, compare your version with Lawrence's:
—were you right?
—what did you learn about the structure of the poem through this exercise?

Praise Of A Collie   *Norman MacCaig*

'burn': a Scots word for stream

Questions to discuss

Compare the two similes used in the poem—'like a proper sea-dog' and 'like a piece of black wind'. Why did Normal MacCaig include them? What effect does the last stanza have?

Compare this poem to 'In Praise of a Young Man' and 'To a Young Lady' (p 78) and then attempt your own poem 'in praise of' some thing, animal or person.

Late Night Walk Down Terry Street   *Douglas Dunn*

Terry Street in Hull is now demolished. It gave the title for Douglas Dunn's first volume of poems.

Questions to discuss

What do the images of the first stanza suggest? Look particularly at the words 'low-powered', 'crackles' and 'yellows': as well as being a straightforward description of the scene, there is a distinct feeling conveyed. What is it? Is it sustained through the poem as a whole?

You might like to try writing a poem about a street near you. Start with the raw material of observations and from your notes build up a picture of the street, as Dunn has done. Choose your words carefully to create a particular feel to the poem.

Nature   *H. D. Carberry*

There are not 'seasons' in the West Indies in the same sense as there are in Britain, North America, Australia, New Zealand or Japan because of the position of the West Indies within the Tropic of Cancer. Instead, there are the variations suggested in Carberry's poem.

If anyone in the class knows the tropics, he or she might like to try a poem conveying the feel of the seasons there. The class as a whole could attempt writing about seasonal changes in cities (they are noticeable if you observe carefully!), in the countryside or in between.

Camping Provençal   *Peter Reading*

'Provençal': of or in Provence, a region in the South of France
This poem is what is known as a 'found' poem: that is to say, the poet found it 'ready-made', as a notice at a camping site. All he has done is to arrange it more carefully on the page to draw attention to its lunacies.

Questions to discuss
In pairs or small groups, read the poem to make sure you 'get' the humour. What is it, do you think, that makes the poem humorous?

This poem should alert you to the possibilities of poetic language in advertisements and notices. Perhaps the best source is advertisements in magazines, which often carry fairly lengthy text. You could compose a display on your classroom wall, drawing particular attention to metaphorical* and extraordinary uses of language in the advertisements.

Section 2
Telling

Extract page from Brouillard du Pont du Tolbiac

Leo Malet/Tardi

© *Casterman 1982*

*I*f the incantation or the magic spell was the first poem, we may be sure that the ballad or rhyming tale, spoken or sung, was quick to follow. The primitive need to be told, or to tell, a story is something buried deep within all of us. It is as true and undying in our sophisticated century as it was the moment the earliest ballad was conjured out of the mind and put together.

In a very real sense, all poems—and works of art in every form—tell a story. The incidents and thoughts they embody sometimes may lie far below the surface: a kind of hidden treasure for all to find. It should always be remembered that there is much more to a poem (its echoes, resonances, reverberations in the reader's mind and imagination) than the mere words printed on the page.

True poets write poems because they must. It is a compulsion almost impossible to ignore. Once some vague notion of theme and subject have been arrived at, there is then the absorbing problem of getting the piece, so to speak, into its right suit of clothes. Should the result be a lyric, a sonnet, or perhaps a form invented by the individual poet? Should it rhyme, or be in free verse? Certainly, form and content should lie together as easily and comfortably as can be managed: and if this is achieved at all, it is invariably by a process of trial and error. But to be a poet without patience is perhaps not to be a poet at all.

As for the way in which a tale may be told, we find (since life and language, the raw materials of poetry, are constantly subject to change) that many narrative forms have been developed and refined since the days of the traditional ballad and story poem. But in the best of their kind, their virtues remain the same: clarity, economy of expression, an absence of moralising and sentimentality. It should be a tale told in such a way that its situations and events speak plainly for themselves. The poet remains neutral; avoids a particular point of view.

In this way, with luck, we may learn a little more of ourselves, of each other, and of the always mysterious world we live in. A good story poem tells us much more than a story, and we should never be deceived by the simplicity with which it may be expressed. The business of poetry is not to answer questions, but to ask them. The rest lies with us: its readers and sharers.

CHARLES CAUSLEY

37

Nursery Rhyme Of Innocence And Experience

I had a silver penny
   And an apricot tree
And I said to the sailor
   On the white quay

'Sailor O sailor
   Will you bring me
If I give you my penny
   And my apricot tree

'A fez from Algeria
   An Arab drum to beat   *10*
A little gilt sword
   And a parakeet?'

And he smiled and he kissed me
   As strong as death
And I saw his red tongue
   And I felt his sweet breath

'You may keep your penny
   And your apricot tree
And I'll bring your presents
   Back from sea.'   *20*

O, the ship dipped down
   On the rim of the sky
And I waited while three
   Long summers went by

Then one steel morning
   On the white quay
I saw a grey ship
   Come in from sea

Slowly she came
   Across the bay   *30*
For her flashing rigging
   Was shot away

All round her wake
   The seabirds cried
And flew in and out
   Of the hole in her side

Slowly she came
   In the path of the sun
And I heard the sound
   Of a distant gun   *40*

And a stranger came running
   Up to me
From the deck of the ship
   And he said, said he

'O are you the boy
   Who would wait on the quay
With the silver penny
   And the apricot tree?

'I've a plum-coloured fez
   And a drum for thee   *50*
And a sword and a parakeet
   From over the sea.'

'O where is the sailor
   With bold red hair?
And what is that volley
   On the bright air?

'O where are the other
   Girls and boys?
And why have you brought me
   Children's toys?'

                                                  60

Charles Causley

An Attitude Of Mind

Heat bounced off the cobbled yard
And hit us in the eyes, already bleared
By the sun to a constant blink.
Starlings showered down on to the barn,
Dipped through the door, paused, and sprayed up again,
Ceaselessly. Dust twirled slowly; a tractor stank.

Tod took a tennis racket, and flicked
It from hand to hand. You've picked
A good time, he said. I'll demonstrate.
The barn was heavy with hay smell   *10*
And all in it invisible
When Tod swung the doors together, tight.

In the dimness hovered small echoings,
The whirring motors of starlings' wings,
Soft and confusing, and right up.
Where the nests were, raucous twitters.
We stood till things assembled round us,
Colouring themselves and taking shape:

A spiked machine, blue plastic sacks
Of nitro-chalk, a couple of hayforks,   *20*
A three-wheeled pram. Heavy beams
Hung over us, streaked white like the walls
Up at the top amid squalls
Of bird noise. Tod flung wide his arms

And shook his muscles loose, and took
A good grip on his racket. With a kick
He broke some pebbles free, and flung one
Up at the roof, then another, then more,
And they clunked about on the wood up there
Before the sharp drop back onto stone.   *30*

And down came the starlings, beating about
In a bewildered way, at head height and waist height,
Dozens of them, whizzing so close they missed
Us by the width of their wind. Tod was using
The racket, swinging from the shoulder, not pausing
At all, grunting and moving very fast.

40

Blow after blow vibrated those strings.
Bodies rocketed to stillness, and there were shufflings
And dragging movements everywhere,
As birds, beaks broken, necks half-unscrewed,   *40*
Flapped untidily and slowly clawed
A small circular progress on the floor.

Tod stamped on these but others escaped to the roof
In the end and sat safe. Tod gave a laugh
At his last few futile swipes and looked
Round at the litter of feathers, at the wrecks
Of birds and bits of birds, at the marks
On the walls where birds had split and cracked.

The nearest bodies he nudged with the toe of his boot
To a neat heap, and he scooped with his racket   *50*
Several more to throw in; he was deft, accurate.
Hungry nests wheezed still. They'll soon starve,
That lot, Tod said, stroking his ear with the curve
Of his racket. Tomorrow in here will be dead quiet.

He opened the doors and the daylight fell
In, hot and dazzling. A good haul,
He said, licking sweat, wiping an eye, puzzled
At my silence. Pests they are from the minute they hatch.
It's all an attitude of mind. He raised an arm to scratch.
Down the words Dunlop Junior dark blood drizzled.   *60*

John Cassidy

As I Walked Out One Evening

As I walked out one evening,
Walking down Bristol Street,
The crowds upon the pavement
Were fields of harvest wheat.

And down by the brimming river
I heard a lover sing
Under an arch of the railway:
'Love has no ending.

'I'll love you, dear, I'll love you
Till China and Africa meet   *10*
And the river jumps over the mountain
And the salmon sing in the street.

'I'll love you till the ocean
Is folded and hung up to dry
And the seven stars go squawking
Like geese about the sky.

'The years shall run like rabbits
For in my arms I hold
The Flower of the Ages
And the first love of the world.'   *20*

But all the clocks in the city
Began to whirr and chime:
'O let not Time deceive you,
You cannot conquer Time.

'In the burrows of the Nightmare
Where Justice naked is,
Time watches from the shadow
And coughs when you would kiss.

'In headaches and in worry
Vaguely life leaks away,   *30*
And Time will have his fancy
To-morrow or to-day.

'Into many a green valley
Drifts the appalling snow;
Time breaks the threaded dances
And the diver's brilliant bow.

'O plunge your hands in water,
Plunge them in up to the wrist;
Stare, stare in the basin
And wonder what you've missed.   *40*

'The glacier knocks in the cupboard,
The desert sighs in the bed,
And the crack in the tea-cup opens
A lane to the land of the dead.

'Where the beggars raffle the banknotes
And the Giant is enchanting to Jack,
And the Lily-white Boy is a Roarer
And Jill goes down on her back.

'O look, look in the mirror,
O look in your distress;   *50*
Life remains a blessing
Although you cannot bless.

'O stand, stand at the window
As the tears scald and start;
You shall love your crooked neighbour
With your crooked heart.'

It was late, late in the evening,
The lovers they were gone;
The clocks had ceased their chiming
And the deep river ran on.   *60*

W. H. Auden

La Belle Dame Sans Merci

O what can ail thee, knight at arms,
    Alone and palely loitering?
The sedge has withered from the lake,
    And no birds sing!

O what can ail thee, knight at arms,
    So haggard and so woe-begone?
The squirrel's granary is full,
    And the harvest's done.

I see a lily on thy brow,
    With anguish moist and fever dew;   *10*
And on thy cheeks a fading rose
    Fast withereth too.'

I met a lady in the meads,
    Full beautiful, a faery's child;
Her hair was long, her foot was light,
    And her eyes were wild.

I made a garland for her head,
    And bracelets, too, and fragrant zone;
She looked at me as she did love,
    And made sweet moan.   *20*

I set her on my pacing steed,
    And nothing else, saw all day long;
For sidelong would she bend, and sing
    A faery's song.

She found me roots of relish sweet,
    And honey wild, and manna dew;
And sure in language strange she said,
    "I love thee true."

She took me to her elfin grot
    And there she wept and sighed full sore;   *30*
And there I shut her wild, wild eyes
    With kisses four.

And there she lullèd me asleep,
  And there I dreamed, ah woe betide!
The latest dream I ever dreamt,
  On the cold hillside.

I saw pale kings, and princes too,
  Pale warriors, death-pale were they all,
Who cried, 'La Bell Dame sans Merci
  Thee hath in thrall!   40

I saw their starved lips in the gloam
  With horrid warning gaped wide—
And I awoke and found me here,
  On the cold hill's side.

And this is why I sojourn here,
  Alone and palely loitering;
Though the sedge is withered from the lake
  And no birds sing.

John Keats

Night Of The Scorpion

I remember the night my mother
was stung by a scorpion. Ten hours
of steady rain had driven him
to crawl beneath a sack of rice.
Parting with his poison—flash
of diabolic tail in the dark room—
he risked the rain again.
The peasants came like swarms of flies
and buzzed the Name of God a hundred times
to paralyse the Evil One.   10
With candles and with lanterns
throwing giant scorpion shadows
on the mud-baked walls
they searched for him: he was not found.
They clicked their tongues.
With every movement that the scorpion made
his poison moved in Mother's blood, they said.
May he sit still, they said.
May the sins of your previous birth
be burned away tonight, they said.   20
May your suffering decrease
the misfortunes of your next birth, they said.
May the sum of evil
balanced in this unreal world
against the sum of good
become diminished by your pain.
May the poison purify your flesh
of desire, and your spirit of ambition,
they said, and they sat around
on the floor with my mother in the centre,   30
the peace of understanding on each face.

More candles, more lanterns, more neighbours,
more insects, and the endless rain.
My mother twisted through and through
groaning on a mat.
My father, sceptic, rationalist,
trying every curse and blessing,
powder, mixture, herb and hybrid.
He even poured a little paraffin

upon the bitten toe and put a match to it.   *40*
I watched the flame feeding on my mother.
I watched the holy man perform his rites
to tame the poison with an incantation.
After twenty hours
it lost its sting.

My mother only said
Thank God the scorpion picked on me
and spared my children.

Nissim Ezekiel

White Child Meets Black Man

She caught me outside a London
suburban shop, I like a giraffe
and she a mouse. I tried to go
but felt she stood
lovely as light on my back.

I turned with hello
and waited. Her eyes got
wider but not her lips.
Hello I smiled again and watched.

She stepped around me   *10*
slowly, in a kind of dance,
her wide eyes searching
inch by inch up and down:
no fur no scales no feathers
no shell. Just a live silhouette,
wild and strange
and compulsive
till mother came horrified.

'Mummy is his tummy black?'
Mother grasped her and swung   *20*
toward the crowd. She tangled
mother's legs looking back at me.
As I watched them birds were singing.

James Berry

47

Emperors Of The Island

There is the story of a deserted island
where five men walked down to the bay.

The story of this island is
that three men would two men slay.

Three men dug two graves in the sand,
three men stood on the sea wet rock,
three shadows moved away.

There is the story of a deserted island
where three men walked down to the bay.

The story of this island is
that two men would one man slay

Two men dug one grave in the sand,
two men stood on the sea wet rock,
two shadows moved away.

There is the story of a deserted island
where two men walked down to the bay.

The story of this island is
that one man would one man slay.

One man dug one grave in the sand,
one man stood on the sea wet rock,
one shadow moved away.

There is the story of a deserted island
where four ghosts walked down to the bay.

The story of this island is
that four ghosts would one man slay.

Four ghosts dug one grave in the sand,
four ghosts stood on the sea wet rock;
five ghosts moved away.

Dannie Abse

Lord Sycamore

I climbed Lord Sycamore's Castle,
The wind was blowing red.
'Top of the morning, my lord,' I cried.
'Top to you,' he said.

'Welcome to Sycamore Castle,'
His smile as sharp as tin,
'Where many broken men come out
That in one piece go in.'

With pusser's eggs and bacon
My belly it was rare.   *10*
'Together,' said Lord Sycamore,
'Let's take the dancing air.'

With a running finger
He chucked me under the chin.
Felt with a lover's quiet hand
Where he might best begin.

Suddenly he cooled me
As we laughed and joked.
Although the month was May, my breath
On the morning smoked.   *20*

On the sum of my body
Lord Sycamore got to work,
Pulled the answer like a rose
Out of my mouth with a jerk.

On Lord Sycamore's Castle
I heard the morning stop;
Over my head, the springing birds,
Under my feet, the drop.

Charles Causley

Ballad Of The Bread Man

Mary stood in the kitchen
Baking a loaf of bread.
An angel flew in through the window.
We've a job for you, he said.

God in his big gold heaven,
Sitting in his big blue chair,
Wanted a mother for his little son.
Suddenly saw you there.

Mary shook and trembled,
It isn't true what you say.   *10*
Don't say that, said the angel.
The baby's on its way.

Joseph was in the workshop
Planing a piece of wood.
The old man's past it, the neighbours said
That girl's been up to no good.

And who was that elegant feller,
They said, in the shiny gear?
The things they said about Gabriel
Were hardly fit to hear.   *20*

Mary never answered,
Mary never replied.
She kept the information,
Like the baby, safe inside.

It was election winter.
They went to vote in town.
When Mary found her time had come
The hotels let her down.

The baby was born in an annex
Next to the local pub.   *30*
At midnight, a delegation
Turned up from the Farmers' Club.

They talked about an explosion
That cracked a hole in the sky,
Said they'd been sent to the Lamb & Flag
To see God come down from on high.

A few days later a bishop
And a five-star general were seen
With the head of an African country
In a bullet-proof limousine. *40*

We've come, they said, with tokens
For the little boy to choose.
Told the tale about war and peace
In the television news.

After them came the soldiers
With rifle and bomb and gun,
Looking for enemies of the state.
The family had packed and gone.

When they got back to the village
The neighbours said, to a man, *50*
That boy will never be one of us,
Though he does what he blessed well can.

He went round to all the people
A paper crown on his head.
Here is some bread from my father.
Take, eat, he said.

Nobody seemed very hungry.
Nobody seemed to care.
Nobody saw the god in himself
Quietly standing there. *60*

He finished up in the papers.
He came to a very bad end.
He was charged with bringing the living to life.
No man was that prisoner's friend.

There's only one kind of punishment
To fit that kind of a crime.
They rigged a trial and shot him dead.
They were only just in time.

They lifted the young man by the leg,
They lifted him by the arm,   *70*
They locked him in a cathedral
In case he came to harm.

They stored him safe as water
Under seven rocks.
One Sunday morning he burst out
Like a jack-in-the-box.

Through the town he went walking.
He showed them the holes in his head.
Now do you want any loaves? he cried.
Not today, they said.   *80*

Charles Causley

Misfortunes Never Come Singly

Making toast at the fireside,
Nurse fell in the grate and died;
And what makes it ten times worse,
All the toast was burnt with nurse.

Harry Graham

Fable

Once upon a time
there was a lonely wolf
lonelier than the angels.

He happened to come to a village.
He fell in love with the first house he saw.

Already he loved its walls
the caresses of its bricklayers.
But the windows stopped him.

In the room sat people.
Apart from God nobody ever   *10*
found them so beautiful
as this child-like beast.

So at night he went into the house.
He stopped in the middle of the room
and never moved from there any more.

He stood all through the night, with wide eyes
and on into the morning when he was beaten to death.

János Pilinszky
Translated by Ted Hughes

53

Her Dancing Days

Those old tunes take me back. I used to go
to dances every Saturday. Of course
I wasn't never going to give it up,
and nor was Lily Cannon, but we did.
We wasn't taught, we just picked up the steps.
In Summer there was dances in Brent Park;
they called them 'flannel dances': out of doors.
The men could wear grey flannels, not the girls.
I used to make my dresses, buy the stuff
up Cricklewood, and sew them in a day.   *10*
I liked the winter-evening dances best,
and used to dance with Horace—he was tall,
and we danced well together—Percival—
he was a butler, rather serious—
Jack Roach, Jack Young, and I forget who else;
but there was one I used to like, and then
one Saturday he wasn't there, and I
was heartbroke. Then he wrote.
I was to meet him at the Bald Faced Stag
one Sunday afternoon. We'd never met   *20*
by day. I didn't like the looks of him.
And Horace was engaged. Then, at a fair
with Lil, she was all out for a good time,
we met these two. One of them wore a cap.
I don't like caps. 'I'll have him then,' said Lil:
all four slid down the helter-skelter, then
the heel come off me shoe; I had to hop;
he fixed it for me. Later, we arranged
to meet again next evening at the Hyde.
    Lily come round, and sat down by the fire   *30*
to knit. 'I'm going out,' I said; 'You're not,
it's raining.' But I was. I had to go.
We didn't know each other's names,
or where we worked, or anything.
And there he waited for me, in the wet,
and fifty years began.
    I said I'd never give up dancing, and
he said the same of football, but we did;

54

and Lily gave up dancing too, quite soon.
   We was both seventeen.   *40*

Anna Adams

Disillusion

Look at him, over there
Watch him turn his head and stare
I think he fancies me

See the way he turns around
See him look me up and down
I'm sure he fancies me

Look at his lovely jet black hair
I don't really like 'em fair
I just know he fancies me

He's coming over, aint he great   *10*
He's gonna ask me for a date
I knew he fancied me

Hang on a minute though
He's heading straight for my
        mate Flo
And I thought he fancied me

Tara Flo, I'll go on home
I spose I really should have known
He didn't fancy me

I don't like un anyway   *20*
He's ugly
I don't fancy he

Maureen Burge

Friedrich

Friedrich, at twenty-two,
Sumptuously bankrupt,
Bought a garage:
Every fuel-tank ailing.

Also a mobilization
Of motor-bikes. Owes
A butcher's ransom
Of Deutschmarks. Has bikes

In the bathroom, kitchen,
Closets, bedroom.   *10*
To use the landing lavatory you have
To aim between two Suzukis.

He's a graceful mover; slim as
A fern-tree. Has a dancer's
Small bottom. His wife Peachy's
A sorceress. They don't

Say much when I'm around
But I know they've something
Going between them better than
Collected Poems, a T.S.B. account,   *20*

Twelve lines in *Gems*
Of Modern Quotations
And two (not war) medals.
Today, Friedrich

Sat for three hours
Earthed by the ears
To a Sony Sound System.
I couldn't hear

The music, only
Him singing. It was like   *30*
A speared hog. *Love*,
Skirled Friedrich, *'s when a cloud*

Fades in the blue
'N there's me, 'n there's you.
'N it's true.
Peachy brings in coke

And Black Forest *gâteau.*
Their mutual gaze
Broaches each other's eye.

Next week he'll be Vasco da Gama.   *40*

Charles Causley

An Incident At Christmas

The old man shuffled round the shop, and
When I asked 'May I help you?' he said
'Last year we bought our presents here,
This year my wife is dead.'

I stammered the words of sympathy, while
Shoppers wrapped up in their own busy lives
Had their purchases wrapped, and didn't see him
Who only saw husbands and wives.

Thelma Barlow

The Pigs

My grey-eyed father kept pigs on his farm
In Tuscany. Like troubled bowels all night
They muttered in my childhood dreams, and grumbled
Slovenly in moonlight, sprawled in night-slush,
While chill winds dried the mud upon their hides.
I lay in the faint glow of oil-lamps,
In a musk-scented stillness,
And from the icy paddocks heard the pigs.

My thoughts were haunted by pig-greed, how pigs
Surge to their food-troughs, trample on each other,   *10*
And grunt and clamber swilling themselves full.
Often we emptied food on top of them,
So that they swam in muck. And then one day
When the wind splattered us with dust, my father
Heard a pig squealing, crushed beneath the press,
And we began to stone the pigs, and drew
Blood with our stones, but they just shook their buttocks,
And grunted, and still tore at cabbage leaves.

Passing a dozing boar one summer morning
My father pointed at two dead-pan eyes   *20*
Which rolled up quizzing me (and yet its head
And snout snoozed motionless, and flies
Fed and hopped undisturbed among the bristles).
Only a pig, my father now explained,
Could glance out of the corner of its eye.
I watch two bead-eyes turn and show
Their whites like death-flesh.

One dusk this huge old boar escaped and chased
Me through an olive-grove upon a hillside.
Dumpy, it thundered after me,   *30*
With murder in its eyes, like someone damned,
A glow of Hades perfuming the air.
That night my father took me in his arms
And told me that of all the animals
Only pigs knew of death

And knew we merely fattened them for slaughter.
Puddles of hatred against man, they wallowed
In greed, despair and viciousness,
Careless of clinging slops and vegetables scraps,
And the sows even eating their own young. *40*
The knowledge of death made pigs into pigs.

Later that year this old boar ate
A peasant woman's baby and was burned
Alive one night by public ceremony.
My father stood there by my side,
His toga billowing in the rush of heat,
But in the flames my child-eyes saw
Not a pig, but myself,
Writhing with stump-legs and with envious eyes
Watching the men who calmly watched my death. *50*

Geoffrey Lehmann

The Ballad Of Charlotte Dymond

Charlotte Dymond, a domestic servant aged eighteen, was murdered near Rowtor Ford on Bodmin Moor on Sunday, 14th April 1844, by her young man, a crippled farm-hand, Matthew Weeks, aged twenty-two. A stone marks the spot.

It was a Sunday evening
   And in the April rain
That Charlotte went from our house
   And never came home again.

Her shawl of diamond redcloth,
   She wore a yellow gown,
She carried the green gauze handkerchief
   She bought in Bodmin town.

About her throat her necklace
   And in her purse her pay: *10*
The four silver shillings
   She had at Lady Day.

In her purse four shillings
   And in her purse her pride
As she walked out one evening
   Her lover at her side.

Out beyond the marshes
   Where the cattle stand,
With her crippled lover
   Limping at her hand.   *20*

Charlotte walked with Matthew
   Through the Sunday mist,
Never saw the razor
   Waiting at his wrist.

Charlotte she was gentle
   But they found her in the flood
her Sunday beads among the reeds
   Beaming with her blood.

Matthew, where is Charlotte,
    And wherefore has she flown?   *30*
For you walked out together
    And now are come alone.

Why do you not answer,
    Stand silent as a tree,
Your Sunday worsted stockings
    All muddied to the knee?

Why do you mend your breast-pleat
    With a rusty needle's thread
And fall with fears and silent tears
    Upon your single bed?   *40*

Why do you sit so sadly
    Your face the colour of clay
And with a green gauze handkerchief
    Wipe the sour sweat away?

Has she gone to Blisland
    To seek an easier place,
And is that why your eye won't dry
    And blinds your bleaching face?

'Take me home!' cried Charlotte,
    'I lie here in the pit!   *50*
A red rock rests upon my breasts
    And my naked neck is split!'

Her skin was soft as sable,
    Her eyes were wide as day,
Her hair was blacker than the bog
    That licked her life away.

Her cheeks were made of honey,
    Her throat was made of flame
Where all around the razor
    Had written its red name.   *60*

As Matthew turned at Plymouth
About the tilting Hoe,
The cold and cunning Constable
Up to him did go:

'I've come to take you, Matthew,
Unto the Magistrate's door.
Come quiet now, you pretty poor boy,
And you must know what for.'

'She is as pure,' cried Matthew,
As is the early dew,   *70*
Her only stain it is the pain
That round her neck I drew!

'She is as guiltless as the day
She sprang forth from her mother.
The only sin upon her skin
Is that she loved another.'

They took him off to Bodmin,
They pulled the prison bell,
They sent him smartly up to Heaven
And dropped him down to Hell.   *80*

All through the granite kingdom
And on its travelling airs
Ask which of these two lovers
The most deserves your prayers.

And your steel heart search, Stranger,
That you may pause and pray
For lovers who come not to bed
Upon their wedding day,

But lie upon the moorland,
Where stands the sacred snow   *90*
Above the breathing river,
And the salt sea-winds go.

Charles Causley

The Castaways or Vote For Caliban

The Pacific Ocean—
A blue demi-globe.
Islands like punctuation marks.

A cruising airliner,
Passengers unwrapping pats of butter.
A hurricane arises,
Tosses the plane into the sea.

Five of them, flung on to an island beach,
Survived.

Tom the reporter.   10
Susan the botanist.
Jim the high-jump champion.
Bill the carpenter.
Mary the eccentric widow.

Tom the reporter sniffed out a stream of drinkable water.
Susan the botanist identified a banana tree.
Jim the high-jump champion jumped up and down and gave
                                   them each a bunch.
Bill the carpenter knocked up a table for their banana supper.
Mary the eccentric widow buried the banana skins,
But only after they had asked her twice.   20
They all gathered sticks and lit a fire.
There was an incredible sunset.

Next morning they held a committee meeting.
Tom, Susan, Jim and Bill
Voted to make the best of things.
Mary, the eccentric widow, abstained.

Tom the reporter killed several dozen wild pigs.
He tanned their skins into parchment
And printed the Island News with the ink of squids.

Susan the botanist developed new strains of banana   30
Which tasted of chocolate, beefsteak, peanut butter,
Chicken and bootpolish.

63

Jim the high-jump champion organized organized games
Which he always won easily.

Bill the carpenter constructed a wooden water wheel
And converted the water's energy into electricity.
Using iron ore from the hills, he constructed lampposts.

They all worried about Mary, the eccentric widow,
Her lack of confidence and her—
But there wasn't time to coddle her.   *40*

The volcano erupted, but they dug a trench
And diverted the lava into the sea
Where it formed a spectacular pier.
They were attacked by pirates but defeated them
With bamboo bazookas firing
Sea-urchins packed with home-made nitro-glycerine.
They gave the cannibals a dose of their own medicine
And survived an earthquake thanks to their skill in jumping.

Tom had been a court reporter
So he became the magistrate and solved disputes.   *50*
Susan the Botanist established
A university which also served as a museum.
Jim the high-jump champion
Was put in charge of law-enforcement—
Jumped on them when they were bad.
Bill the carpenter built himself a church,
Preached there every Sunday.

But Mary the eccentric widow . . .
Each evening she wandered down the island's main street,
Past the Stock Exchange, the Houses of Parliament,   *60*
The prison and the arsenal.
Past the Prospero Souvenir Shop,
Past the Robert Louis Stevenson Movie Studios,
Past the Daniel Defoe Motel
She nervously wandered and sat on the end of the pier of lava,

Breathing heavily,
As if at a loss,
As if at a lover,
She opened her eyes wide
To the usual incredible sunset.   *Adrian Mitchell*

Notes and activities

Nursery Rhyme Of Innocence And Experience   *Charles Causley*

Nursery rhymes are usually spoken and this poem, like many others benefits from being read aloud. First read it carefully to yourself, becoming aware of the three voices in the poem, before it is read aloud.

Questions to discuss

Why do you think Charles Causley called this poem 'Nursery Rhyme of Innocence and Experience'? It may help you to understand the poem if you:
   —think about how the poem is like a nursery rhyme
   —look at the changes which happen—to the speaker, the sailor and the ship
   —list the images which suggest innocence (such as a fez, a drum) and those which suggest experience.
What does the poem suggest about childhood and growing up?

Either: write a prose piece about the changes that have happened to you since you were a small child. Do you feel differently about anything? Have you changed your ideas about what is important to you, about what makes you happy or unhappy, about what you want from life?
Or: write a poem about your early childhood, concentrating on what you thought and felt at a particular age. You might, as Causley has done, use images of toys or other objects to convey a vivid picture of your childhood world.

An Attitude Of Mind   *John Cassidy*

Questions for discussion
(in pairs)

Read this poem to yourself very carefully before considering the following questions which you might like to work at in pairs:

1   What contrast is there in stanza 1 between the natural world and things that men make?
2   Where in the next three stanzas is this contrast repeated? What contrast do you think is more effective? Why?
3   What details in stanzas 8 and 9 are particularly horrifying?
4   What phrase or sentence in stanza 9 suggests that Tod had done this before?

5   When we look back at stanza 2, which word is particularly ominous and how is it given particular emphasis?
6   How does he justify what he has done?

Now look at 'The Pigs' by Geoffrey Lehmann. Both these poems are about human cruelty to animals. Make notes on the similarities and differences that you notice between the two poems. You might consider, for example:
   —where the poems are set
   —the attitudes of the speaker in the poems
   —the contrasts between men and nature
   —words and phrases that are particularly effective
   —the tone* of each poem
Discuss your notes in groups or as a class and then write a comparison of the two poems.

As I Walked Out One Evening   *W. H. Auden*
'seven stars' (1.15): usually the planets or The Pleiades (a group of stars) or The Great Bear (a constellation)

Questions to discuss
As you read the poem to yourself, try to decide how many speakers there are and how the poem might be best read.
This poem contains many difficult lines which may make it hard, at first reading, to have any idea of what the poem is about. It may help you to consider and then discuss the following statements:
1   Lines 9–16: the promises of the lover are deliberately silly.
2   Lines 18–20: the statement of the lover is sincere and moving.
3   Lines 23–44: time is seen as the destroyer of love.
4   Lines 33–34: the 'green valley' symbolises love and the 'appalling snow' symbolises time.
5   Lines 41–44 brilliantly suggest death is everywhere.
6   Lines 45–48 suggest that the world we live in is the opposite of the world of fairy tales and nursery rhymes.
7   Lines 55–56 suggest that love is neither grand nor good.
Having read these statements do you think the poem is about:
   —the lasting quality of love
   —that the real enemy of love is time
   —how weak human love really is?

Invent some more promises or statements that the lover of lines 8–20 might make, trying to make some ridiculous and some sincere.

La Belle Dame Sans Merci *John Keats*

The title is French and means 'The beautiful lady without pity'.
'sedge' (l.3): a coarse grass   'zone' (1.18): a belt
'manna' (1.26): food, usually given by God
'grot' (1.29): cave   'thrall' (1.40): enthralled

Questions to discuss
This is a ballad* poem which tells a story about two characters, a knight and a lady. Discuss, in pairs or small groups:
The knight: what do the words 'loitering' and 'alone and pale' suggest about him?
La belle dame: what details suggest she is not really human?
The setting: what time of year is it? How does this affect the mood of the poem? (Think about how the poem would be different if set on a beautiful summer's day.)
Keat's purpose in writing this poem: Why do you think he wrote about a knight and a lady and not about ordinary people? What do you think he wanted us to feel? Do you think the rhythm* and rhyme help him to achieve his purpose?

'La Belle Dame Sans Merci' is a poem which involves the supernatural or the dark side of magic. Write your own supernatural or magical poem, keeping in mind the importance of setting, the way Keats uses formal, old-fashioned language and the rhyme and rhythm which are typical of the ballad.

Night Of The Scorpion *Nissim Ezekiel*

Questions to discuss
There are three attitudes to the scorpion's bite in this poem: decide *whose* they are and *what* they are. What religious faith do you think the villagers belong to: how does this affect the attitude of the peasants; the poet's father? Are the peasants and the father really concerned about the mother? Who is the mother concerned about?

This poem is beautifully observed and told in a very flat, undramatic manner. Try writing a poem about an illness or injury in this way. Express your and others' attitudes and concentrate on rhythm.

White Child Meets Black Man *James Berry*

Before you read this poem, write a short piece or a poem with the same title. You might concentrate on what each of them sees and on what each of them thinks and feels.

Questions to discuss
After a careful reading of Berry's poem, read over your own writing. What are the strengths of each? What does the girl in Berry's poem expect the poem's

speaker to be like? What does her question make her mother feel? How does the speaker feel?

If you now feel you can improve your own piece of writing, rework or even rewrite it.

Emperors Of The Island   *Dannie Abse*

Questions to discuss
How many examples of repetition can you find in this poem? What effect is achieved by this repetition?
Bearing in mind the title, do you think this poem has anything to say about power, corruption or greed?

Look back at Keats' poem 'La Belle Dame Sans Merci'. Make notes on the similarities and differences between these two poems. You might like to consider: the poet's intention; mood; setting; vocabulary; rhythm and rhyme.

Lord Sycamore   *Charles Causley*

'pusser's': naval issue

Questions to discuss
What is the story being told here? What should first alert us to the fact that Lord Sycamore's castle is not a pleasant place?

Write the story in your own words. What does it gain and what does it lose from being written in prose?

Ballad Of The Bread Man   *Charles Causley*

Before you read this poem, make sure you know the story of Jesus Christ's life.
Read the poem aloud, then read it carefully to yourself.
Write down your immediate response. You might note lines which puzzle you as well as words and phrases which stand out for one reason or another.

Statements for discussion
Now consider the truth of the following statements. Make sure you have reasons and references to the poem for agreeing or disagreeing with them.

1   This poem is not set at any particular time.
2   All the people in the poem seem unpleasant and selfish.
3   This poem suggests that modern life is full of war and violence.
4   This poem mocks the idea of God and religion.
5   Stanza 16 suggests that people are not really alive.
6   The poem suggests that there can be no justice in this world.
7   The poem suggests that people do not want to be helped.

Bearing in mind your first responses and your answers to the above questions, write a full response to the poem: what is Causley suggesting about the world and how effectively does he express his ideas and feelings?

You might also, as Causley as done, take a traditional story and bring it up to date. You could write it in prose before trying to write it as a ballad. Concentrate more on a regular rhythm than on rhyme.

Misfortunes Never Come Singly   *Harry Graham*
Questions to discuss
This poem tells a story that is meant to be funny. What makes it funny? Is the alliteration* important?

Fable   *János Pilinszky (translated from the Hungarian by Ted Hughes)*
Read the poem aloud.
Read it again, to yourself, twice.
It's called 'Fable'. What is a fable?

Questions for discussion
(in pairs)
1   How many folk stories and fables can you recall that are about wolves? How do we normally think of wolves in fables?
2   This wolf is 'lonelier than the angels'. How do we think of angels? How do we now think of the wolf?
3   What do the facts that the wolf was 'lonely' and 'fell in love' make us feel about the wolf?
4   'caresses' of its bricklayers—why that word? What does it tell us about the wolf and his feelings?
5   What does 'childlike' tell us about the wolf? What if that word were 'childish'?
    Do we think the children and angels (see question 2) have anything in common? What?
6   Why is he beaten to death?

When you have discussed these questions, consider the following questions as a class:
7   How is this poem like a fable?
8   Most fables have morals. If this poem were to have a moral, what would it be?
9   What does the wolf represent?

Take a folk-tale or a fable and rewrite it in condensed form, in a similar style to this poem.

Her Dancing Days   *Anna Adams*
Disillusion   *Maureen Burge*
Read both these poems carefully to yourself.
In 'Her Dancing Days', Brent Park and Cricklewood are areas of London.

Questions to discuss
These poems are dramatic monologues*. Think about how you could read
them aloud, especially the final lines. What differences and similarities can
you see in these two poems, especially in the characters of the two speakers
and what they say?

*Write a dramatic monologue which tells a story. It might be about something
you've done, seen or read. You might take a story from a newspaper and
imagine you've been involved in it. Make your writing conversational rather
than strictly accurate and try to reveal the sort of person the speaker is—it
need not be you!*

Friedrich   *Charles Causley*
'Deutschmarks' (1.8): German money
'T.S.B.' (1.20): the Trustee Savings Bank
'Vasco da Gama' (1.38): a famous Portugese navigator, born in the 15th
century

Questions to discuss
How would you describe the character written about in this poem? Explain
the contrast between the man he is and the man he would like to be. What
effect is achieved by keeping the last line separate?

*Who would you like to be? Try writing as if you were that person, but living the
life you lead. Concentrate on the embarrassing and amusing consequences of
imagining you are someone else.*

Incident At Christmas   *Thelma Barlow*
Questions to discuss
The key to this poem is in lines 6–8. What two meanings does the word
'wrapped' have here? Think about why, now, the other shoppers do not see
the old man and why he only sees 'husbands and wives'. What criticism is this
poem making of our world?

Write the poem out as a paragraph of prose. Note down or discuss in pairs:
   —what differences you can see between the poem and the paragraph
   —the effects created by the rhymes and the layout of the lines
   —the words or phrases given emphasis by the poem

The Pigs   *Geoffrey Lehmann*
'Tuscany' (l.2): an area of Italy
'Hades' (l.32): an ancient Greek name for Hell
'toga' (l.46): an ancient Roman robe, worn by most Romans

Questions to discuss
What is the attitude of the speaker and his father to the pigs in lines 1–46?
How does the speaker's attitude change in the last four lines? What is
happening to the speaker in these last lines?

*This poem tells a story about human cruelty to animals. You might try writing
a poem or prose-piece about this subject. Concentrate on one incident—you
may know stories about cruelty committed by hooligans, hunters or scien-
tists—and, like Geoffrey Lehmann, describe the incident objectively before
revealing your own feelings.*

The Ballad Of Charlotte Dymond   *Charles Causley*
Questions to discuss
   'Ask which of these two lovers
   The most deserves your prayers'
How has Causley told this story so that the question he poses at the end is
difficult to answer?

The Castaways or Vote For Caliban   *Adrian Mitchell*
Caliban: a character in Shakespeare's play *The Tempest* who represents
'uncivilised' man. He is usually thought of as being brutal and savage.
Prospero: another character in *The Tempest* who represents order and
'civilisation'
Robert Louis Stevenson: the author of *Treasure Island*
Daniel Defoe: the author of *Robinson Crusoe*

Questions to discuss
What do the five characters do on the island? What is the attitude of the
others to Mary, and what do the last five lines suggest about Mary?
On one level, Mitchell is telling a straightforward story, but he also raises
questions in the reader's mind about what we would call 'civilisation'. Discuss
what you think these questions are.

*Write an extract from an imaginary diary kept by one of the five characters.
You could include your feelings about the other four, recording the things
you might like or dislike about them. Think particularly about Mary: what
should be done about her and what might happen to her eventually.
A dramatised reading from the different diaries could be interesting!*

71

Section 3
Transforming

Study for Portrait
Francis Bacon

*I*f you were walking along the shore, for instance, and saw an object of a kind you had never seen before, how would you describe it? Obviously you would have to describe it in terms of something else. You would have to say, 'It was like . . . well, it was like . . .'

Poets however do this with ordinary objects and they do this because poets more than most people see the objects of the world with a fresh eye.

Burns sang, 'My love is like a red red rose,' and he was thinking of the lady's freshness, fragrance, dewy-fresh beauty. Modern songs are sometimes less flattering, for instance we hear of 'eyes like custard pies'.

The poet makes the world a continuous surprise. Ah, you thought this was a hosepipe but I think it's like a snake, he says. And so in front of your eyes hovers the image of hosepipe and snake together. Of course the hosepipe is not venomous but water pours out of it and it is long and sinuous.

In the section now before us we see poets doing this. The atomic bomb is like an animal that you dare not touch, dare not provoke, and this makes us see the bomb in a new way. The gunner is in the belly of the State: first of all he was in the belly of his mother, now he is in the belly of a plane and the plane reflects the power of the state. And what is the 'wet fur'? Well, it is the wetness of the new born child but also it is the wet fur of the airman flying high above the earth in cold moisture. In one poem there is an apple with a red coat and in another a colour-blind person seeing green blood.

These transformations, these surprises . . . why are they done? They are done because this is the way the poet sees the world. It is part of his being as a poet. Even in early poetry and stories we see this happening. Animals become men, men become animals. Women change into seals, seals back into women. The poet in a sense is a miracle-maker. Our Lord changed water into wine. On a lesser level, conjurors dip into their bags and take out a handkerchief which changes into a dove. Poets are conjurors. In the eyes of a poet a toad may look like a purse, or a boat like a rocking cradle. This is what we call metaphor. And it is what the great philosopher Aristotle thought distinguished the true poet from the inferior one. It is the power of seeing deep into things and finding resemblances where we had thought there were only differences. It is in the end a unifying power.

IAIN CRICHTON SMITH

The World's A Minefield

The world's a minefield when I think of you.
I must walk carefully in case I touch
some irretrievable and secret switch
that blows the old world back into the new.

How careless I once was about this ground
with the negligence of ignorance. Now I take
the smallest delicate steps and now I look
about me and about me without end.

Iain Crichton Smith

The Death Of The Ball Turret Gunner

From my mother's sleep I fell into the State
And I hunched in its belly till my wet fur froze.
Six miles from earth, loosed from its dream of life,
I woke to black flak and the nightmare fighters.
When I died they washed me out of the turret with a hose.

Randall Jarrell

Atomic Bomb

This is the bomb. Look at it.
It's napping. Please
do not provoke it
with canes, rods, sticks, thorns,
rocks. Feeding
is prohibited.
Careful with your hands,
your eyes!

(The Director
has said it and given notice,   10
but no one pays any attention,
not even the Minister.)

A very great danger
this animal here.

Nicolas Guillen

On Certain Survivors

When the man
Was dragged out from under
The debris
Of his shelled house,
He shook himself
And said:
Never again.

At least, not right away.

Bertolt Brecht

O What Is That Sound

O what is that sound which so thrills the ear
  Down in the valley, drumming, drumming?
Only the scarlet soldiers, dear,
  The soldiers coming.

O what is that light I see flashing so clear
  Over the distance brightly, brightly?
Only the sun on their weapons, dear,
  As they step lightly.

O what are they doing with all that gear,
  What are they doing this morning, this morning?   *10*
Only their usual manoeuvres, dear,
  Or perhaps a warning.

O why have they left the road down there,
  Why are they suddenly wheeling, wheeling?
Perhaps a change in their orders, dear.
  Why are you kneeling?

O haven't they stopped for the doctor's care,
  Haven't they reined their horses, their horses?
Why, they are none of them wounded, dear,
  None of these forces.   *20*

O is it the parson they want, with white hair,
  Is it the parson, is it, is it?
No, they are passing his gateway dear,
  Without a visit.

O it must be the farmer who lives so near.
  It must be the farmer so cunning, so cunning?
They have passed the farmyard already, dear,
  And now they are running.

O where are you going? Stay with me here!
  Were the vows you swore deceiving, deceiving?   *30*
No, I promised to love you, dear,
  But I must be leaving.

O it's broken the lock and splintered the door,
　　O it's the gate where they're turning, turning;
Their boots are heavy on the floor
　　And their eyes are burning.

W. H. Auden

The Apple's Song

Tap me with your finger,
rub me with your sleeve,
hold me, sniff me, peel me
curling round and round
till I burst out white and cold
from my tight red coat
and tingle in your palm
as if I'd melt and breathe
a living pomander
waiting for the minute　　　　　　　　　　　　　10
of joy when you lift me
to your mouth and crush me
and in taste and fragrance
I race through your head
in my dizzy dissolve.

I sit in the bowl
in my cool corner
and watch you as you pass
smoothing your apron.
Are you thirsty yet?　　　　　　　　　　　　　20
My eyes are shining.

Edwin Morgan

In Praise Of A Young Man

Young man, you are
A hare that ascends a hill running,
A rope that drags the elephant along,
A lion that kills the tiger,
A head that never touches the ground,
A log of the *inyi* wood.

To A Young Lady

Young lady, you are
A mirror that must not go out in the sun,
A child that must not be touched by dew,
One that is dressed up in hair,
A lamp with which people find their way,
A moon that shines bright,
An eagle-feather worn by a husband,
A straight line drawn by God.

I Dunno

I sometimes think I'd rather crow
And be a rooster than to roost
And be a crow. But I dunno.

A rooster he can roost also,
Which don't seem fair when crows can't crow
Which may help some. Still I dunno.

Crows should be glad of one thing though;
Nobody thinks of eating crow,
While roosters they are good enough
For anyone unless they're tough.   *10*

There's lots of tough old roosters though,
And anyway a crow can't crow,
So mebby roosters stand more show.
It looks that way. But I dunno.

Anon

Proverbs

A lie has short legs.

You need a lot of spades to bury truth.

When your enemy is an ant, fear him like a lion.

Sit crooked, but talk straight.

You can't block out the sun with your hand.

If there were no wind, cobwebs would cover the sky.

When it thunders, each man is afraid of himself.

Even the sun goes through mud, but it doesn't get dirty.

He gets in your eyes like sweat.

A wolf pays with his skin.

Measure a wolf's tail when he's dead.

Even his tail is a burden to a tired fox.

Vasko Popa

Uncle Edward's Affliction

Uncle Edward was colour-blind;
We grew accustomed to the fact.
When he asked someone to hand him
The green book from the window-seat
And we observed its bright red cover
Either apathy or tact
Stifled comment. We passed it over.
Much later, I began to wonder
What a curious world he wandered in,
Down streets where pea-green pillar boxes   10
Grinned at a fire-engine as green;
How Uncle Edward's sky at dawn
And sunset flooded marshy green.
Did he ken John Peel with his coat so green
And Robin Hood in Lincoln red?
On country walks avoid being stung
By nettles hot as a witch's tongue?
What meals he savoured with his eyes:
Green strawberries and fresh red peas,
Green beef and greener burgundy.   20
All unscientific, so it seems:
His world was not at all like that,
So those who claim to know have said.
Yet, I believe, in war-smashed France
He must have crawled from neutral mud
To lie in pastures dark and red
And seen, appalled, on every blade
The rain of innocent green blood.

Vernon Scannell

What Kind Of Guy Was He?

Just so you shouldn't have to ask again,
He was the kind of guy that if he said
Something and you were the kind of guy that said
You can say that again, he'd say it again.

Howard Nemerov

Metaphors

I'm a riddle in nine syllables,
An elephant, a ponderous house,
A melon strolling on two tendrils.
O red fruit, ivory, fine timbers!
This loaf's big with its yeasty rising.
Money's new-minted in this fat purse.
I'm a means, a stage, a cow in calf.
I've eaten a bag of green apples,
Boarded the train there's no getting off.

Sylvia Plath

Magic Words (after Nalungiaq)

In the very earliest time,
when both people and animals lived on earth,
a person could become an animal if he wanted to
and an animal could become a human being.
Sometimes they were people
and sometimes animals
and there was no difference.
All spoke the same language.
That was the time when words were like magic.
The human mind had mysterious powers.   *10*
A word spoken by chance
might have strange consequences.
It would suddenly come alive
and what people wanted to happen could happen—
all you had to do was say it.
Nobody could explain this:
That's the way it was.

Eskimo

The Language Of Shamans

Say the leash	*& mean* the father
„ where things get soft	„ the guts
„ soup	„ a seal
„ what makes me dive in	
headfirst	„ a dream
„ what cracks your ears	„ a gun
„ a jumping thing	„ a trout
„ what keeps me standing	
straight	„ your clothes
„ little walker	„ a fox
„ walker with his head down	„ a dog
„ the bag it lies in	„ a mother
„ the bag it almost lies in	„ a stepmother
„ a person smoke surrounds	„ a live one
„ a floating one	„ an island
„ a flat one	„ a wolf
„ a shadow	„ a white man
„ he turned my mind around	„ he told me something

Eskimo

The River God

I may be smelly and I may be old,
Rough in my pebbles, reedy in my pools,
But where my fish float by I bless their swimming
And I like the people to bathe in me, especially women.
But I can drown the fools
Who bathe too close to the weir, contrary to rules.
And they take a long time drowning
As I throw them up now and then in a spirit of clowning.
Hi yih, yippity-yap, merrily I flow,
O I may be an old foul river but I have plenty of go.   *10*
Once there was a lady who was too bold
She bathed in me by the tall black cliff where the water runs cold,
So I brought her down here
To be my beautiful dear.
Oh will she stay with me will she stay
This beautiful lady, or will she go away?
She lies in my beautiful deep river bed with many a weed
To hold her, and many a waving reed.
Oh who would guess what a beautiful white face lies there
Waiting for me to smooth and wash away the fear   *20*
She looks at me with. Hi yih, do not let her
Go. There is no one on earth who does not forget her
Now. They say I am a foolish old smelly river
But they do not know of my wide original bed
Where the lady waits, with her golden sleepy head.
If she wishes to go I will not forgive her.

Stevie Smith

Notes and activities

The World's A Minefield   *Iain Crichton Smith*
'irretrievable': not able to be found again
'the negligence of ignorance': 'negligence' is irresponsible carelessness.

Questions to discuss
For discussion in small groups:
—who the 'you' mentioned in line 1 might be
—why the poet uses the words 'the old world back into the new' and not the other way round
—what was the speaker 'ignorant' of earlier in the relationship?

Either: follow a single metaphor through to the end of a poem of your own devising. Another example of this use of language is Shakespeare's 'All the world's a stage . . .' (in As You Like It *Act II Sc 7).*
Or: use the situation described in the poem as a basis for a story or dramatic sketch.

The Death Of The Ball Turret Gunner   *Randall Jarrell*
'ball turret': a revolving armoured position on a bomber aeroplane

Questions to discuss
This poem reads almost like a riddle (compare it with 'Metaphors' on page 81). Can you identify the features that give it that feel? Indeed it *is* a bit of a puzzle. Try to work it out in small groups, looking at what is meant and suggested by:
'my mother's sleep'
'the State'
'my wet fur'
'they washed me out of the turret with a hose'.
The 'answer' to the riddle is given in the title.

Atomic Bomb   *Nicolas Guillen*
Nicolas Guillen is a Cuban poet and this poem comes from his collection called *The Great Zoo.* Each poem represents the notice on the cage which we read as Guillen takes us on a tour of the zoo. But this is no ordinary zoo: it houses, among other things, The Caribbean, a guitar, rivers, thirst and hunger, cancer and the moon. The zoo, then, is a metaphor for all aspects of human life and experience.

Questions to discuss
What does the metaphor of the zoo suggest about the world and how we live?

Create your own 'Great Zoo'. Some ideas for exhibits that aren't contained in Guillen's zoo are: love, school, war, birds, envy and television. Anything can go in. Make sure you not only capture your subject, but also the style of the announcement on each cage. This is not only good practice in directed writing, but a fine opportunity for a wall display—or even a model—of your work.

On Certain Survivors   *Bertolt Brecht*

Brecht was a radical German dramatist and poet. The rise of Nazism in Germany in the 1920s and 1930s forced him to emigrate to America. He eventually settled in East Germany.

Questions to discuss

What is the man's attitude at the end of the poem? What is it he is 'never again' going to do, and why does he qualify it with 'At least, not right away'?

Write out this poem as prose, then experiment with various line lengths. What is lost by rearranging the lines? Why has Brecht set it out like this?

O What Is That Sound   *W. H. Auden*

This poem is ideal for reading aloud in pairs, or in larger groups. The reading needs some rehearsal, and once the poem has been read quietly to yourself several times, you should at least answer these questions before you start to read it aloud:

Questions for discussion
(in pairs or small groups)

1   Are the answers (the third and fourth lines of each stanza) all spoken by the same person?
2   If so, is the person a man or woman?
3   Whom is he or she speaking to?
4   Does the questioner's tone change throughout the poem? Could it?
5   Does the answerer's tone change at all? How is 'dear' to be said?
6   Why does the answerer leave in the penultimate (last but one) stanza?
7   Who speaks the last two lines?
8   What is happening in that final stanza?
9   What sound effects might help a reading of the poem?
10   What is this poem getting at?

You could record your reading, and/or present it to the class.

Which other poems in this book are good for reading aloud?
What did you learn about the poem and about poetry in general by rehearsing a reading of it.

The Apple's Song   *Edwin Morgan*
This poem is another example of a personified subject
'pomander': a ball of perfumes

Questions to discuss
Why is there a break between 'dissolve' and the last six lines?

*Write an essay comparing this poem with 'The River God'. You should give a
detailed account of how each poem works, discuss the effect of personification in the poems, and say which poem you find the more effective—and why.*

In Praise Of A Young Man
To A Young Lady   *Oral poems*
These Igbo poems from Eastern Nigeria are fine examples of metaphorical
writing. 'Inyi' wood is exceptionally hard.

Questions to discuss
What qualities of character are being emphasised in each poem?

*Try writing your own poem 'in praise of' another person: a friend, or perhaps
someone you admire.*

Proverbs   *Vasko Popa*
These are Yugoslavian proverbs collected by Vasko Popa.

Questions to discuss
Can you think of (a) other proverbs and (b) other kinds of language that are
metaphorical like this? Discuss the proverbs in small groups, trying to tease
out their meanings. What is particularly appropriate—or inappropriate—
about the image used to convey the message? Can you think of examples to
illustrate the proverbs?

*You might like to use one of the proverbs as the title to a poem, play or story
of your own.*

Uncle Edward's Affliction   *Vernon Scannell*
Questions to discuss
What do red and green usually signify? What is the significance of the last five
lines and why does the poem end there? Is the poem humorous or serious or
both?

*What is the most striking thing about this poem: the memory of Uncle Edward
or the exploration of colour blindness? You might use this poem as a starting
point for your own writing: exploring the associations of various colours, or
painting a portrait of an older member of your family with memories 'before
your time'.*

Metaphors   *Sylvia Plath*

Plath here is making a series of statements about herself in the form of comparisons. What makes the poem seem hard to grasp is that the comparisons seem unclear and not connected to one another. However, the following questions, which you might consider in pairs, may help you towards an understanding of the poem.

Questions for discussion
(in pairs)

1   What is Plath suggesting by writing that she is a 'riddle'? Would a riddle in so many syllalbes be easy or hard to guess?
2   What does an 'elephant' have in common with a 'ponderous' house?
3   What shape is a melon? Does this fit in with the two previous comparisons? To what, in real life, do the 'tendrils' refer?
4   To what, in the poem, do the 'red fruit, ivory, fine timbers' refer back?
5   The fact that Plath refers to herself as a loaf 'big with rising' should, together with the previous comparisons, give you a clue to her physical condition when she wrote the poem. Consider also line 7, a 'cow in calf'.
6   What, then, does money 'new-minted' refer to?
7   In what sense is Plath a 'means' and a 'stage'? A means to what and a stage between what two things?
8   How would eating a 'bag of green apples' make you feel? Is this appropriate?
9   Would the last line have a different effect if there were a full stop after 'Boarded the train'?
10   Which metaphors imply that Plath is happy about her state and which suggest that she is not so pleased?

Plath might simply have written, 'I am pregnant and I feel fat and heavy'. Would this have been more effective? Give your reasons.

Write some comparisons, similes or metaphors, about yourself which indicate your feelings about yourself at various times. Don't forget that we all usually think of ourselves as being both better and worse than we actually are.

Magic Words   *Nalungiaq*

Questions to discuss

The poem talks about the time when people and animals shared the same language. What do you notice about the language of *this* poem? How is it different from the language of the shamans or Vasko Popa's 'Proverbs'? Which kind of language do you find the most powerful?

There is enormous possibility here for using the poem as a basis for dramatic exploration. Take some of the lines as a starting point: for example, 'a person could become an animal if he wanted to' or 'A word spoken by chance/might have strange consequences'.

The Language Of Shamans   *Anon (Eskimo)*
'shaman': witch doctor or 'spirit-man'

These riddle-like transformations give the language of the shamans a peculiar power. See if you can create further examples of such language. That 'the leash' suggests 'the father' says something very distinct about the shaman's (writer's) view of the father; you could equally choose a happier image, like 'Say the sun and mean the father'. What does each image suggest about the person, creature or thing to which it refers.

The River God   *Stevie Smith*
This is the first of two poems where the *persona* or speaker of the poem is the thing itself: in this case, the river. The river is 'personified', or given human qualities.

Questions to discuss
What personality does the river have?
What is the tone of this poem? How can you tell?

Write a poem in which an animal, natural or artificial subject 'speaks'. It need not be in the same tone as 'The River God'.

Section 4
Reflecting

A Bigger Splash
David Hockney

A poet is expected to go beyond a reflection of real experience, whether the poet's own or someone else's. We expect a poet to help us to a little of that special knowledge of life that comes through poetry, even if only through a memorable or musical arrangement of words.

You might wonder what that special knowledge is. Readily enough, we admit that poetry often gives us insights that clarify experience or help us to understand. But prose does that, too, or drama, or the cinema, or music. What is special about poetry is not a knowledge that exists simply as information. Instead, it is a knowledge of mood, often imprecise, inexact, suggesting more than it tells; not, strictly speaking, factual, but working through imaginative recognitions of real things and states of being, and very often open enough for the reader to allow a poem to be added to by his or her own meditations.

Reflecting, meditating, thinking, dreaming, remembering—in poetry, these descriptions of mind can often happen together, and can be added to by the observation of real things, nature, creatures, people, streets. In the way I read poetry, it seems to me that two lines in Gary Snyder's 'Hay for the Horses' might illustrate what I mean.

'—The old mare nosing lunch-
    pails,
Grasshoppers crackling in the
    weeds—'

Snyder prints the lines almost in parentheses, as if they might be unimportant, a quick sketch of background. Yet if you can see and hear the scene, the clarity of the poem becomes alive and warm. Not only do you see and hear the old man and what he discloses about his life, but you feel the mood in which he speaks.

I call that mood 'lyric'. Not all poetry-thinking is or should be lyrical, but a lot of it is. It is a mood that dispels moralising or a tendency to shut the reader out of the poem with an underlined conclusion, the sort of finality that denies experience its mysteries. It provokes thought; it does not deny the reader of the poem the pleasures of thinking for himself or herself. In other words, a reflective or thoughtful poem need not be, and perhaps ought not to be, one that imposes a poet's thought on a reader. Instead, it invites the reader to enter the poet's mind, to see what has been seen, feel what was felt, and experience the poet's response to what encouraged the poem into being.

DOUGLAS DUNN

The Building Site

In a haze of brick dust
and red sun
All day
The men slog.
Lumbering about
The curled ridges of clay
In clod-hopping boots
Humping brick hods
On the brawn of red shoulders
Up piped and rattling scaffolding   *10*
And uneven boards
To where their mates
With deft flicks from trowels
Make house walls grow
Brick by red brick.
All day too
The great trucks bang and clatter
Back and forth
And the churning mixer
Slops out gobs of concrete   *20*
In wholesome pats
Onto the dusty earth.

At twelve
They break up,
Swarming from scaffolding
To drink brown tea
From huge mugs
That they grip in the beef of their fists.
After,
They kick a ball about   *30*
Or lie and bronzie in the sun
Till it's turn-to time again.

The afternoon shift wears on:
They whistle more
Shout out and laugh
And sing the songs that blare
From two transistors.

At six
They knock off
And pack into a lorry   *40*
With their clobber.
Down the rutted track they bound
Shouting and cheering.
When the dust and pandemonium clears
The shells of houses,
workmanless, stand
Still.
Silence
In the settling haze.
A sparrow bounces on rubble   *50*
A curious mongrel snuffles
On an inspection tour.

I wouldn't mind being a labourer
For a bit.

Gareth Owen

Does It Matter?

Does it matter?—losing your legs? . . .
For people will always be kind,
And you need not show that you mind
When the others come in after hunting
To gobble their muffins and eggs.

Does it matter?—losing your sight? . . .
There's such splendid work for the blind;
And people will always be kind,
As you sit on the terrace remembering
And turning your face to the light.   *10*

Do they matter?—those dreams from the pit? . . .
You can drink and forget and be glad,
And people won't say that you're mad;
For they'll know you've fought for your country
And no one will worry a bit.

Siegfried Sassoon

Hay For The Horses

He had driven half the night
From far down San Joaquin
Through Mariposa, up the
Dangerous mountain roads,
And pulled in at eight a.m.
With his big truckload of hay
       behind the barn.
With winch and ropes and hooks
We stacked the bales up clean
To splintery redwood rafters
High in the dark, flecks of alfalfa   10
Whirling through shingle-cracks of light,
Itch of haydust in the
       sweaty shirt and shoes.
At lunchtime under Black oak
Out in the hot corral,
—The old mare nosing lunchpails,
Grasshoppers crackling in the weeds—
'I'm sixty-eight' he said,
'I first bucked hay when I was seventeen
I thought, that day I started,
I sure would hate to do this all my life   20
And dammit, that's just what
I've gone and done.'

Gary Snyder

Differences

Distressed, I hear a name called out:
Not mine.

Relieved,

I hear a name called out:
Not mine.

Günter Kunert

Tonight At Noon

(for Charles Mingus and the Clayton Squares)

Tonight at noon
Supermarkets will advertise 3d EXTRA on everything
Tonight at noon
Children from happy families will be sent to live in a home
Elephants will tell each other human jokes
America will declare peace on Russia
World War I generals will sell poppies in the streets on
     November 11th
The first daffodils of autumn will appear
When the leaves fall upwards to the trees

Tonight at noon   *10*
Pigeons will hunt cats through city backyards
Hitler will tell us to fight on the beaches and on the landing fields
A tunnel full of water will be built under Liverpool
Pigs will be sighted flying in formation over Woolton
and Nelson will not only get his eye back but his arm as well
White Americans will demonstrate for equal rights
in front of the Black House
and the Monster has just created Dr Frankenstein

Girls in bikinis are moonbathing
Folksongs are being sung by real folk   *20*
Artgalleries are closed to people over 21
Poets get their poems in the Top 20
Politicians are elected to insane asylums
There's jobs for everyone and nobody wants them
In back alleys everywhere teenage lovers are kissing
in broad daylight
In forgotten graveyards everywhere the dead will quietly
bury the living
and
You will tell me you love me
Tonight at noon   *30*

Adrian Henri

Science, Where Are You?

I started smoking young. The Big C
didnt scare me. By the time
I was old enough to get it,
Science would have found the cure.
'Ad astra per angina' was the
family motto, and thrombosis
an heirloom I didn't care to inherit.
But I didn't worry. By the time
I was old enough to face it
St Science would surely have   *10*
slain that particular dragon.

Suddenly I'm old enough . . .
Science, where are you Science?
What have you been doing
all these years? Were you playing
out when you should have been
doing your homework? Daydreaming
in class when you should
have been paying attention?
Have you been wasting your time   *20*
and worse still, wasting mine?

When you left school did you
write scripts for 'Tomorrow's World'
before being seduced by a starlet
from a soap ad? Lured by the
bright lights of commercialism
did you invent screwtop bottles,
self-adhesive wallpaper, nonstick
pans, chocolate that melts
in the mouth not the hands?   *30*
Kingsize fags, tea-leaves in bags
cars and bras sycophantic
Oxo cubes now transatlantic?

(Or worse still
did you fall
for a sweet talkin'
warmonger? Have a
consciencectomy
and practise
death control?)   *40*

The Arts I expected nothing from.
Good company when they're sober
but totally unreliable. But
Science, I expected more from you.
A bit dull perhaps, but steady.
Plodding, but getting there in the end.
Now the end limps into view
and where are you? Cultivating
cosmic pastures new? Biting off
more Space than you can chew?   *50*
Science you're needed here, come down
and stay. I've got this funny pain
and it won't go awa
                       a
                       a
                        a
                         g
                          g
                         g
                           h
                            h
                           h

Roger McGough

97

Warning

When I am an old woman I shall wear purple
With a red hat which doesn't go, and doesn't suit me,
And I shall spend my pension on brandy and summer gloves
And satin sandals, and say we've no money for butter.
I shall sit down on the pavement when I'm tired
And gobble up samples in shops and press alarm bells
And run my stick along the public railings
And make up for the sobriety of my youth.
I shall go out in my slippers in the rain
And pick the flowers in other people's gardens   *10*
And learn to spit.

You can wear terrible shirts and grow more fat
And eat three pounds of sausages at a go
Or only bread and pickle for a week
And hoard pens and pencils and beermats and things in boxes.

But now we must have clothes that keep us dry
And pay our rent and not swear in the street
And set a good example for the children.
We will have friends to dinner and read the papers.

But maybe I ought to practise a little now?   *20*
So people who know me are not too shocked and surprised
When suddenly I am old and start to wear purple.

Jenny Joseph

September In Great Yarmouth

The woodwind whistles down the shore
Piping the stragglers home; the gulls
Snaffle and bolt their final mouthfuls.
Only the youngsters call for more.

Chimneys breathe and beaches empty,
Everyone queues for the inland cold—
Middle-aged parents growing old
And teenage kids becoming twenty.

Now the first few spots of rain
Spatter the sports page in the gutter.   *10*
Council workmen stab the litter.
You have sown and reaped; now sow again.

The band packs in, the banners drop,
The ice-cream stiffens in its cone.
The boatman lifts his megaphone:
'Come in, fifteen, your time is up.'

Derek Mahon

Inspection

'You! What d'you mean by this?' I rapped.
'You dare come on parade like this?'
'Please sir, it's'—'Old yer mouth,' the sergeant snapped.
'I take 'is name, sir?'—'Please, and then dismiss.'

Some days 'confined to camp' he got
for being 'dirty on parade'.
He told me afterwards, the damned spot
Was blood, his own. 'Well, blood is dirt,' I said.

'Blood's dirt,' he laughed, looking away
Far off to where his wound had bled   10
And almost merged for ever into clay.
'The world is washing out its stains,' he said.
'It doesn't like our cheeks so red.
Young blood's its great objection.
But when we're duly white-washed, being dead,
The race will bear Field-Marshal God's inspection.'

Wilfred Owen

Breakfast

We ate our breakfast lying on our backs
Because the shells were screeching overhead.
I bet a rasher to a loaf of bread
That Hull United would beat Halifax
When Jimmy Stainthorpe played full-back instead
Of Billy Bradford. Ginger raised his head
And cursed, and took the bet, and dropt back dead.
We ate our breakfast lying on our backs
Because the shells were screeching overhead.

W. W. Gibson

Thin Ice

Walking in February
A warm day after a long freeze
On an old logging road
Below Sumas Mountain
Cut a walking stick of alder,
Looked down through clouds
On wet fields of the Nooksack—
And stepped on the ice
Of a frozen pool across the road.
It creaked   *10*
The white air under
Sprang away, long cracks
Shot out in the black,
My cleated mountain boots
Slipped on the hard slick
—like thin ice—the sudden
Feel of an old phrase made real—
Instant of frozen leaf,
Icewater, and staff in hand.
'Like walking on thin ice—'   *20*
I yelled back to a friend.
It broke and I dropped
Eight inches in

Gary Snyder

The River-Merchant's Wife: A Letter

While my hair was still cut straight across my forehead
I played about the front gate, pulling flowers.
You came by on bamboo stilts, playing horse,
You walked about my seat, playing with blue plums.
And we went on living in the village of Chōkan:
Two small people, without dislike or suspicion.

At fourteen I married My Lord you.
I never laughed, being bashful.
Lowering my head, I looked at the wall.
Called to, a thousand times, I never looked back.   10

At fifteen I stopped scowling,
I desired my dust to be mingled with yours
For ever and for ever and for ever.
Why should I climb the look out?

At sixteen you departed,
You went into far Ku-tō-yen, by the river of swirling eddies,
And you have been gone five months.
The monkeys make sorrowful noise overhead

You dragged your feet when you went out.
By the gate now, the moss is grown, the different mosses,   20
Too deep to clear them away!
The leaves fall early this autumn, in wind.
The paired butterflies are already yellow with August
Over the grass in the West garden;
They hurt me. I grow older.
If you are coming down through the narrows of the river Kiang,
Please let me know beforehand,
And I will come out to meet you
                    As far as Chō-fū-Sa.

Li Po [Rihaku]
Translated from the Chinese by Ezra Pound

A Song Of Ch'ang-kan

(*Written to music*)

My hair had hardly covered my forehead.
I was picking flowers, playing by my door,
When you, my lover, on a bamboo horse,
Came trotting in circles and throwing green plums.
We lived near together on a lane in Ch'ang-kan,
Both of us young and happy hearted.
. . . At fourteen I became your wife,
So bashful that I dared not smile,
And I lowered my head toward a dark corner
And would not turn to your thousand calls;   *10*
But at fifteen I straightened my brows and laughed,
Learning that no dust could ever seal our love,
That even unto death I would await you by my post
And would never lose heart in the tower of silent watching.
. . . Then when I was sixteen, you left on a long journey
Through the Gorges of Ch'ü-t'ang, of rock and whirling water.
And then came the Fifth-month, more than I could bear,
And I tried to hear the monkeys in your lofty far-off sky.
Your footprints by our door, where I had watched you go,
Were hidden, every one of them, under green moss,   *20*
Hidden under moss too deep to sweep away.
And the first autumn wind added fallen leaves.
And now, in the Eighth-month, yellowing butterflies
However, two by two, in our west-garden grasses. . . .
And, because of all this, my heart is breaking
And I fear for my bright cheeks, lest they fade.
. . . Oh, at last, when you return through the three Pa districts,
Send me a message home ahead!
And I will come and meet you and will never mind the distance,
All the way to Chang-fêng Sha.

Sunday Morning Among The Houses Of Terry Street

On the quiet street, Saturday night's fag-packets,
Balls of fish and chip newspaper, bottles
Placed neatly on window sills, beside cats.

A street of oilstains and parked motorbikes,
Wet confectionery wrappers becoming paste,
Things doing nothing, ending, rejected.

Revellers return tieless, or with hairdo's deceased,
From parties, paying taxis in the cold,
Unsmiling in the fogs of deflated mirth.

Neighbours in pyjamas watch them from upstairs,   10
Chewing on pre-breakfast snacks,
Waiting for kettles to boil, wives quit the lav.

Men leave their beds to wash and eat,
Fumble with Sunday papers and radio knobs,
Leaving in their beds their wives and fantasies,

In bedside cups their teeth, their smiles.
Drinkers sleep into a blank sobriety,
Still talking to the faces in the smoke,

Women they regretted they were too drunk to touch,
Sucking tastes in their mouths, their mossy teeth.   20
Into the street come early-risen voices,

The Salvation Army's brass dulled in sunlessness
And breath of singers the colour of tubas.
Dog obbligatos come from warm corners.

Behind the houses, antique plumbing
Coughs and swallows Sunday morning's flush
Down to Hull's underworld, its muddy roots.

The city of disuse, a sink, a place,
Without people it would be like the sea-bottom.
Beneath the street, a thundering of mud.   30

Douglas Dunn

We Wear The Mask

We wear the mask that grins and lies,
It hides our cheeks and shades our eyes—
This debt we pay to human guile;
With torn and bleeding hearts we smile,
And mouth with myriad subtleties.
Why should the world be otherwise,
In counting all our tears and sighs?

Nay, let them only see us while
   We wear the mask.

We smile, but, O great Christ, our cries   *10*
To thee from tortured souls arise.
We sing, but oh the clay is vile
Beneath our feet, and long the mile;
But let the world dream otherwise,
   We wear the mask.

Paul Laurence Dunbar

Sergeant Brown's Parrot

Many policemen wear upon their shoulders
cunning little radios. To pass away the time
They talk about the traffic to them, listen to the news,
And it helps them to Keep Down Crime

But Sergeant Brown, he wears upon his shoulder
A tall green parrot as he's walking up and down
And all the parrot says is 'Who's a-pretty-boy-then?'
'I am,' says Sergeant Brown.

Kit Wright

Catching Up On Sleep

             i go to bed early
             to catch up on my sleep
                         but my sleep
             is a slippery customer
             it bobs and weaves
                         and leaves
             me exhausted. It
side steps my clumsy tackles
             with ease.   Bed
             raggled I drag
             myself to my knees.

             The sheep are countless   *10*
             I pretend to snore
             yearn for chloroform
             or a sock on the jaw
             body sweats heart beats
             there is Panic in the Sheets
             until
             as dawn slopes up the stairs
             to set me free
             unawares
             sleep catches up on me   *20*

Roger McGough

The Grey Squirrel

Like a small grey
coffee-pot,
sits the squirrel.
He is not

all he should be,
kills by dozens
trees, and eats
his red-brown cousins.

The keeper on the
other hand,   10
who shot him, is
a Christian, and

loves his enemies,
which shows
the squirrel was not
one of those.

Humbert Wolfe

'They'

The Bishop tells us: 'When the boys come back
They will not be the same; for they'll have fought
In a just cause: they lead the last attack
On Anti-Christ; their comrades' blood has bought
New right to breed an honourable race,
They have challenged Death and dared him face to face.'

'We're none of us the same!' the boys reply.
'For George lost both his legs; and Bill's stone blind;
Poor Jim's shot through the lungs and like to die;
And Bert's gone syphilitic: you'll not find   10
A chap who's served that hasn't found *some* change.'
And the Bishop said: 'The ways of God are strange!'

Siegfried Sassoon

107

'Out, Out—'

The buzz saw snarled and rattled in the yard
And made dust and dropped stove-length sticks of wood,
Sweet-scented stuff when the breeze drew across it.
And from there those that lifted eyes could count
Five mountain ranges one behind the other
Under the sunset far into Vermont.
And the saw snarled and rattled, snarled and rattled,
As it ran light, or had to bear a load.
And nothing happened; day was all but done.
Call it a day, I wish they might have said   *10*
To please the boy by giving him the half hour
That a boy counts so much when saved from work.
His sister stood beside them in her apron
To tell them 'Supper'. At the word, the saw,
As if to prove saws knew what supper meant,
Leaped out at the boy's hand, or seemed to leap—
He must have given the hand. However it was,
Neither refused the meeting. But the hand!
The boy's first outcry was a rueful laugh,
As he swung toward them holding up the hand   *20*
Half in appeal, but half as if to keep
The life from spilling. Then the boy saw all—
Since he was old enough to know, big boy
Doing a man's work, though a child at heart—
He saw all spoiled. 'Don't let him cut my hand off—
The doctor, when he comes. Don't let him, sister!'
So. But the hand was gone already.
The doctor put him in the dark of ether.
He lay and puffed his lips out with his breath.
And then—the watcher at his pulse took fright.   *30*
No one believed. They listened at his heart.
Little—less—nothing!—and that ended it.
No more to build on there. And they, since they
Were not the one dead, turned to their affairs.

Robert Frost

The Jungle Husband

Dearest Evelyn, I often think of you
Out with the guns in the jungle stew
Yesterday I hittapotamus
I put the measurements down for you but they got lost in the fuss
It's not a good thing to drink out here
You know, I've practically given it up dear.
Tomorrow I am going alone a long way
Into the jungle. It is all gray
But green on top
Only sometimes when a tree has fallen   10
The sun comes down plop, it is quite appalling.
You never want to go in a jungle pool
In the hot sun, it would be the act of a fool
Because it's always full of anacondas, Evelyn, not looking ill-fed
I'll say. So no more now, from your loving husband, Wilfred.

Stevie Smith

Notes and activities

The Building Site   *Gareth Owen*
Questions to discuss
How do the labourers seem to feel about their life? Why did Owen place the words 'Still' and 'Silence' (lines 47 and 48) on their own? What is the main contrast in this poem? What is suggested about Owen's feelings towards the labourers' life by the last three words being placed on their own?

Does It Matter?   *Siegfried Sassoon*
Sassoon fought and was wounded on several occasions during the First World War. He argued passionately against the continuance of British involvement in the war, and at one point threw the Victoria Cross he had been awarded for bravery into the River Mersey.

Questions to discuss
What is the tone of this poem: sarcastic, ironic or just bitter?

Prepare various readings of the poem to convey its different shades of meaning.

Hay For The Horses   *Gary Snyder*
San Joaquin and Mariposa are towns in California.

Questions to discuss
Like Owen's 'The Building Site', this poem describes a day's work and one man's reaction to it. Again, there is a contrast between work and leisure. What details make that contrast effective?

Write a poem or prose piece describing what goes on in a building during and after the working day. You might take your school and focus on particular classrooms or areas. Note the way both Owen and Snyder have used specific details to suggest the difference between working and relaxation.

Differences   *Gunter Kunert*
Questions to discuss
Write this poem out as two sentences. What difference does the layout make to the meaning and effect of the poem?

Talk about an occasion when you wished your name had been called out or when you were glad that it wasn't called out. Try to remember the exact circumstances and precisely what you saw, heard and felt.

Tonight At Noon   *Adrian Henri*

Questions to discuss

What do all the details in the first 29 lines have in common? How do we react to the final two lines? Think about what Adrian Henri is suggesting about modern life; about equal rights in America; about folksongs; about art galleries and politicians; about people under 21.

Try writing your own version of this poem. Keep the title and the last three lines, if you like, but create your own ideas and images for the rest of the poem.

Science, Where Are You?   *Roger McGough*

'Ad astra per angina': a parody of the Latin phrase 'per ardua ad astra' (through steepness to the stars) and means 'to the stars through heart disease'

Questions to discuss

Like 'Catching Up On Sleep' this is a comic poem, but it also has a serious theme. What details in the poem are comic and what serious? To what uses has science been put, according to McGough, and to what uses should it have been put?

Write out the poem as an argument. You might begin: When I was young, I didn't worry about cancer . . .
In pairs or small groups, compare your 'prose argument' with the original poem: what do you lose and what do you gain in the prose version?

Warning   *Jenny Joseph*

Questions to discuss

What examples does Joseph give of 'sobriety'? What attitude to life do they suggest? What attitude to life is suggested by the details in lines 1–11? Discuss the contrast between these two attitudes.

Do you know any old people who are in some way odd or eccentric? How do they behave? How ought they to behave, according to 'society'?

September In Great Yarmouth   *Derek Mahon*

Great Yarmouth is a holiday town, one that depends to a large extent on tourism and holidaymakers. Such a town will be very crowded in the summer but will quickly empty once the holiday season is over.

You might read the poem over to yourself before it is read aloud. Read it to yourself carefully, trying to feel the rhythm of the poem, being aware of the rhymes. After hearing it, you may like to break into groups to consider the following questions, before one of you from each group reports back to the class:

111

1 Is the title important? Note what sort of place it is as well as the time of year. Would it make any difference if the poem was set, say, in Birmingham or Florida?

2 Does the weather in the poem suggest anything to you about the mood of the poem? Look particularly at lines 1, 5, 6, 9 and 10. Why does the ice-cream (line 14) 'stiffen'? Is that what you would expect? Does line 11 affect the mood? ('Workmen', 'stab' and 'litter' could all be important.)

3 What other lines or phrases suggest a particular mood or feeling?

4 What lines or phrases are given particular emphasis by alliteration*?

5 Line 12 has echoes of The Bible but it is a more direct reference to some lines by a seventeenth-century writer, Samuel Butler:
> 'As the ancients
> Say wisely, Have a care o'th'main chance,
> And look before you ere you leap;
> For, as you sow, you are like to reap.'

What does this suggest about the way we live and the way we should live?

What does this have to do with other ideas in the poem?

6 What is the main theme* or idea in this poem? Lines 7, 8, 19 and 20 seem very important. Would it be enough to say that the main theme is that all good things must come to an end?

7 How does the weather in the poem, and therefore the mood of the poem, contribute to the main theme?

After studying and discussing this poem, you might like to observe your own town or an area of your city that you know well or even your own school. Write down details of what you see, concentrating on what is significant to you. How does what you see make you feel and think? How does the way you are feeling affect the way you look and think about things? Weather, sounds, colours, textures, shapes, people—the way they walk or sit, the way they look, the clothes they wear, what they are doing—are all important. Does what you see make you happy or sad? Does it depress you or excite you? What events and feelings do you associate with the things you see?

Don't worry at this stage about linking your observations together. Don't worry about rhymes or rhythms or even about writing proper sentences. Think instead about observing accurately and in detail and about your feelings, ideas and mood. Later you might work these observations into a prose paragraph or poem.

Inspection   *Wilfred Owen*

This poem was written during the First World War.

Questions to discuss
The poem presents a conflict between two men. What happens during the poem? Whom does the writer really agree with? Try to see how the images of blood, dirt and washing are developed throughout the poem. What does the last line suggest about (a) God (b) Field-Marshals?

Breakfast   *W. W. Gibson*

Questions to discuss
In pairs or small groups, consider:
—the tone of the poem and its effects
—why Gibson repeats the first two lines at the end
—the contrast between Ginger's death and most of the rest of the poem.

Thin Ice   *Gary Snyder*

Sumas Mountains and Nooksack are in California.

Questions to discuss
The heart of this poem is in the lines:

> '. . . the sudden
> Feel of an old phrase made real'.

What does Snyder mean by this? What realisation has struck him?

The River-Merchant's Wife: A Letter   *Li Po, translated by Ezra Pound*

A Song Of Ch'ang-kan   *Li Po, anonymous translation*

A 'perfect' translation from one language to another is not possible because words are not always equivalent, e.g. French 'brun' = 'brown'. So one translation might bring out certain qualities of an original, and another quite different qualities. One might aim to translate the 'feeling' and another the 'words'. There is no right or wrong way to translate, as long as you remain faithful to the original.

Questions for discussion
Firstly, make a note of what seem to you the most important differences between the two versions.
Secondly, which of these differences affect the meaning of the poem, and how?
Thirdly, which version do you prefer, and why?

If you are studying another language, ask your teacher if you could have a short poem in that language to try and translate. In this way, you will learn the difficulties and rewards of such a project. You will also learn a good deal about writing and about the poet you are working on.

Sunday Morning Among The Houses Of Terry Street *Douglas Dunn*

Questions to discuss

What sort of street is Terry Street and what sort of people live there? In the last stanza, what is suggested about the city by the word 'sink'? What importance does Dunn suggest that people have?

As an exercise in observation, write a poem about your own neighbourhood on a Sunday morning, remembering how much actual observed detail Dunn has included here.

We Wear The Mask *Paul Laurence Dunbar*

'guile': deceit
'myriad'; many and varied

Questions to discuss

In pairs or small groups consider:
  —what the poet suggests that people feel, most of the time
  —the images he uses to suggest those feelings
  —the contrast between what we really feel and what is conveyed by the mask we wear. Is this contrast effective?

Paul Laurence Dunbar is a black American poet. Read the poem again: do you view the poem any differently now?

Write about an incident—a meeting, a conversation, at a party—from two points of view. In the first stanza or paragraph, concentrate on what happened on the surface. In the second, concentrate on your feelings beneath the surface, behind the mask. What were you really feeling? What would you have liked to do or say? You could use two different voices: third person for one point of view and first person for the other.

Sergeant Brown's Parrot *Kit Wright*

Questions to discuss

Why does the phrase 'Keep Down Crime' have three capital letters? Why is the final line so much shorter than the others? Is this just a comic poem or does it suggest anything serious about policemen?

Catching Up On Sleep *Roger McGough*

Questions to discuss

How is sleep presented in lines 4–8? What details show how desperate for sleep McGough is? Are these details wholly serious? At the beginning of the poem, McGough intends to 'catch up on my sleep'. What has changed by the end of the poem?

The Grey Squirrel *Humbert Wolfe*

Questions to discuss

What does the simile in the first two lines make us feel about the squirrel? At what point do you realise that this poem has a moral? Do the poem's short lines and regular rhymes contribute to the poem's effect?

Write the poem out as prose, lengthening the lines and eliminating the rhymes. What differences emerge?

'They' *Siegfried Sassoon*

Questions to discuss

Working in pairs, comment on:
  —the Bishop's attitude to the war
  —the way in which he says the men will have changed
  —the effect of the second stanza
  —why line 7 echoes line 2
  —what Sassoon intends us to feel about the Bishop
  —the tone of the poem.

Write the bishop's diary entries, before and after he meets the returning soldiers.

'Out, Out—' *Robert Frost*

The title is taken from the play *Macbeth*
'buzz saw': a circular saw

Questions to discuss

What is the attitude of the others to the boy's death? How do we feel about his death? What is the speaker's attitude to the incident?

Describe the incident from someone else's point of view—for example, his sister's.

The Jungle Husband *Stevie Smith*

Questions to discuss

What impression do you gain of Wilfred? Are any of the things 'he' writes amusing or strange?

Write another letter from Wilfred to Evelyn or a reply from Evelyn to Wilfred.

Section 5
Childhood

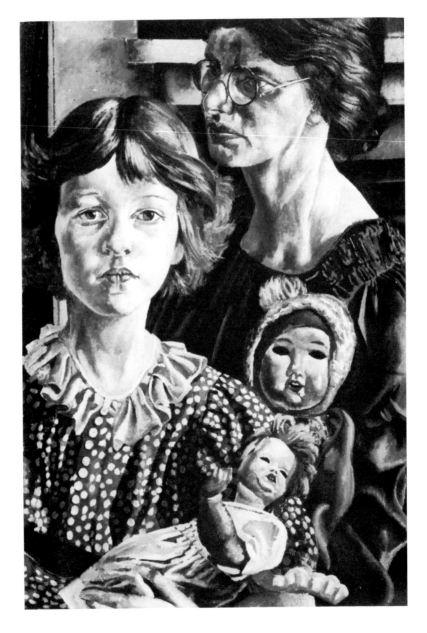

Hilda, Unity and Dolls
Sir Stanley Spencer

When we are children—if we are lucky—we learn how to smile, how to laugh, to make jokes and solve riddles, to fool around and have adventures, to pretend we are cowboys (or cowgirls), nurses, doctors, astronauts, and explorers, to play with animals, and make friends. We also learn how to cry and sulk, to feel afraid, to feel lonely, and to know other forms of distress. And we learn how to make things, to build, to invent, to improvise, to train pets, to organise a den or a bedroom.

We learn that days are never long enough, that the sun sets too quickly, that weekends are too short, that snowmen thaw too quickly, that doors bang on fingers, that flames burn, that electricity shocks.

We learn to forget ourselves, to 'get lost' in an exciting story-book, to wear ourselves to exhaustion by going on too long, to avoid difficult grown-ups, to 'fib' our way out of trouble.

Then, one day, sooner or later, it's all over: a door seems to close behind us, and we know we shall never be able to go back. And later we start to remember, to recall, to revisit our childhood years. And later still we realize that we shall probably never feel anything as intensely as we felt when we were children—neither the pains, nor, alas, the pleasures.

GEOFFREY SUMMERFIELD

Hide And Seek

Call out. Call loud: 'I'm ready! Come and find me!'
The sacks in the toolshed smell like the seaside.
They'll never find me in this salty dark,
But be careful that your feet aren't sticking out.
Wiser not to risk another shout.
The floor is cold. They'll probably be searching
The bushes near the swing. Whatever happens
You mustn't sneeze when they come prowling in.
And here they are, whispering at the door;
You've never heard them sound so hushed before.　　　　　　*10*
Don't breathe. Don't move. Stay dumb. Hide in your blindness.
They're moving closer, someone stumbles, mutters;
Their words and laughter scuffle and they're gone.
But don't come out just yet; they'll try the lane,
And then the greenhouse and back here again.
They must be thinking that you're very clever,
Getting more puzzled as they search all over.
It seems a long time since they went away.
Your legs are stiff, the cold bites through your coat;
The dark damp smell of sand moves in your throat.　　　　　　*20*
It's time to let them know that you're the winner.
Push off the sacks. Uncurl and stretch. That's better!
Out of the shed and call to them 'I've won!'
'Here I am! Come and own up I've caught you!'
The darkening garden watches. Nothing stirs.
The bushes hold their breath; the sun is gone.
Yes, here you are. But where are they who sought you?

Vernon Scannell

Hide And Seek

Children play on into
the summer evening, the block
full of excited shouts.
These girls tied a rope
to the lamp post   higher and higher.
Others sing slightly off-key
counting-out songs, and songs
from TV and Sunday school.
Across the street
                    boys and girls
whoosh by on skate boards   *10*
that rumble to the end of the block.

From trees behind the houses
birds are calling
about the gathering night.
Chicks scramble
among the familiar ordure
loose-clotted in the nest.

In their father's gardens
children are hiding
up in orchard trees, seeking   *20*
to be lost and found.

Mother comes down
for the youngest
and as the dark thickens
for the oldest too.

Indoors, under a naked bulb,
eight puppies sleep
close against the huge hairy body
of their mother. The bees
have returned to their Queen.   *30*
The crescent moon rises
nine-tenths of it still hidden
but imperceptibly moving
below the moving stars
and hugging the earth.

Thom Gunn

Entering The City

The city lies ahead. The vale
is cluttering as the train speeds through.
Hacked woods fall back; the scoop and swell
of cooling towers swing into view.

Acres of clinker, slag-heaps, roads
where lorries rev and tip all night,
railway sidings, broken sheds,
brutally bare in arc-light,

summon me to a present far
from Pericle's Athens, Caesar's Rome,   *10*
to follow again the river's scar
squirming beneath detergent foam.

I close the book, and rub the glass;
a glance ambiguously dark
entertains briefly scrap-yards, rows
of houses, and a treeless park,

Like passing thoughts. Across my head
sundry familiar and strange
denizens of the city tread
vistas I would, and would not, change.   *20*

Birth-place and home! The diesels' whine
flattens. Excited and defiled
once more, I heave the window down
and thrust my head out like a child.

Tony Connor

Dumb Insolence

I'm big for ten years old
Maybe that's why they get at me

Teachers, parents, cops
Always getting at me

When they get at me

I don't hit em
They can do you for that

I don't swear at em
They can do you for that

I stick my hands in my pockets   *10*
And stare at them

And while I stare at them
I think about sick

They call it dumb insolence

They don't like it
But they can't do you for it

I've been done before
They say if I get done again

They'll put me in a home
So I do dumb insolence   *20*

Adrian Mitchell

Poem Of Distant Childhood

When I was born in the great house on the bank of the sea
It was midday and the sun shone on the Indian Ocean.
Sea gulls hovered, white, drunk with blue.
The boats of the Indian fishermen had not yet returned
dragging the overloaded nets.
On the bridge, the cries of the blacks, the blacks of the boats
calling to the married women melting in the heat—
bundles on their heads, street urchins at their sides—
the cries sounded like a long song,
long, suspended in the fog of the silence.   10
And on the scalding steps
beggar Mufasini slept, in a swarm of flies.

When I was born . . .
I know the air was calm, still (they told me)
and the sun shone on the sea.
In the midst of this calm I was launched in the world,
already with my stigma.
And I cried and screamed I don't know why.
Ah, but for the life outside,
my tears dried in the light of revolt.   20
And the sun never again shone as in the first days
of my existence
although the brilliant maritime scenery of my childhood,
constantly calm, like a marsh,
always guided my adolescent steps—
my stigma, too.
And even more, the mixed companions of my childhood.

Companions
fishing under the bridge with a pin hook and line of thin wire
my ragged friends with stomachs round as baskets   30
companions running and jumping in the bush and
beaches of Catembe
together in the marvellous discovery of the nest of the warblers
in the construction of a columned snare
with the sticky sap of the wild fig tree
in the hunt for hummingbirds and blue-headed lizards,
and chasing monkeys under a burning summer sun.
Unforgettable figures as I grew up—

122

Free, happy children:
black, mulatto, white, Indian,   40
sons of the baker and black washerwoman,
of the black man of the boats and the carpenter,
come from the misery of Guachene
or the wooden houses of fishermen.
Coddled children from the post,
smart-aleck sons of the customs guards of Esquadrilla
comrades in the always new adventure
of assaults on the cashew tree in the vegetable gardens,
companions in the secret of the sweetest cones of the pine,
and in the eerie chill of the 'Island of Lost Ships'   50
where every sound makes an echo.

Oh my companions, crouched, amazed in the marvellous
gathering of the 'Karingana wa karingana'
the stories of the old woman from Portugal
in the terrible storm-black sunsets
(the wind shrieking in the zinc roof,
the sea menacing the wooden steps of the veranda,
the causeway groaning, groaning,
inconsolably
and filling our souls with strange, inexplicable fears,   60
our souls full of toothless spirits
and Massinga kings turned hunchbacked . . .)
Yes, my companions sowed in me the seed of this dissatisfaction
day by day I grow more dissatisfied.
They filled my childhood with the sun that shone
on the day I was born.
With their luminous unthinking comradeship,
their radiant happiness,
their explosive enthusiasm before any winged kite
in the technicolor blue of the sky,   70
their immediate, unconditional loyalty—
they filled my childhood
with unforgettable happiness and adventure.

If today the sun does not shine
as on the day I was born
in the great house by the Indian Ocean,
I will not let myself sleep in darkness.
My companions are sure guides

on my life's path
They prove that 'brotherhood' is not a mere pretty word   *80*
written in black in the bookcase dictionary:
They showed me that brotherhood is a beautiful thing and is
    possible
even when skins and surrounding landscapes
differ so much.

So I BELIEVE that one day
the sun will shine again, calm, on the Indian Ocean.
Sea gulls will hover, white, drunk with blue
and the fishermen will return singing,
sailing on the tenuous afternoon.
And this poison of the moon that suffering has infused in my   *90*
veins will cease disturbing me forever.
One day,
life will be flooded with sun.
And it will be like a new childhood shining for everyone . . .

Noémia da Sousa

Translated from Portuguese by Allan Francovich and Kathleen Weaver

Poem For My Sister

My little sister likes to try my shoes,
to strut in them,
admire her spindle-thin twelve-year-old legs
in this season's styles.
She says they fit her perfectly,
but wobbles
on their high heels, they're
hard to balance.

I like to watch my little sister
playing hopscotch, admire the neat hops-and-skips of her,   *10*
their quick peck,
never-missing their mark, not
over-stepping the line.
She is competent at peever.

I try to warn my little sister
about unsuitable shoes,
point out my own distorted feet, the callouses,
odd patches of hard skin.
I should not like to see her
in my shoes.   *20*
I wish she would stay
sure footed,
            sensibly shod.

Liz Lochhead

1945

The news was of inhumanity,
Of crimes, obscenities,
Unspeakable insanity
And bestial atrocities.

Somebody turned the radio down.
Nobody said a word.
Auschwitz, Buchenwald, and Belsen:
'It couldn't happen here,' they said.

At school the teacher set revision:
Of the princes murdered in the tower,   10
The Spanish Inquisition,
And Genghis Khan drunk with power;

Of heretics, burnt at the stake,
Refusing to deny a vow;
Mass-murders for religion's sake;
He said, 'It couldn't happen now.'

'You're next,' the school-bullies snigger,
'Don't try any silly tricks!'
All through History he tries to figure
A way out of punches and kicks.   20

At the end of morning-school,
They drag him to an air-raid shelter.
Down into darkness, damp and cool,
With Puncher and Kicker and Belter.

They tear off all his clothes
And tread them on the floor.
With obscenities and oaths,
They let him have what-for.

Their tortures are very crude,
Clumsy and unrefined.   30
With a sudden change of mood
They pretend to be friendly and kind.

They change their tack once more
And punch him black and blue.
He ends, crouched on the floor,
And finally they're through.

With a special parting kick
They warn him not to talk.
He feels wretched, sore and sick,
Gets up, can hardly walk.   *40*

It's a beautiful Summer day,
His eyes squint in the sun.
He hears two passing women say,
'Oh, schooldays are such fun.'

Words echo in his head:
'Couldn't happen here,' they said.
And 'Couldn't happen now,' they said.
He never breathes a word.

Geoffrey Summerfield

Cowboy

I remember, on a long
Hot, summer, thirsty afternoon
Hiding behind a rock
With Wyatt Earp
(His glasses fastened on with sellotape)

The Sioux were massing for their last attack

We knew

No 7th Cavalry for us
No bugles blaring in the afternoon
I held my lone star pistol in my hand   *10*
Thinking
I was just seven and too young to die
Thinking

Save the last cap
For yourself
                                                   Richard Hill

My Papa's Waltz

The whiskey on your breath
Could make a small boy dizzy;
But I hung on like death:
Such waltzing was not easy.

We romped until the pans
Slid from the kitchen shelf;
My mother's countenance
Could not unfrown itself.

The hand that held my wrist
Was battered on one knuckle;   *10*
At every step you missed
My right ear scraped a buckle.

You beat time on my head
With a palm caked hard by dirt,
Then waltzed me off to bed
Still clinging to your shirt.

Theodore Roethke

Leave-Taking

The only joy
of his old age
he often said
was his grandson

Their friendship
straddled
eight decades
three generations

They laughed, played
quarrelled, embraced
watched television together
and while the rest had
little to say to the old man
the little fellow was
a fountain of endless chatter

When death rattled
the gate at five
one Sunday morning
took the old man away
others trumpeted their
grief in loud sobs
and lachrymose blubber

He never shed a tear
just waved one of his
small inimitable goodbyes
to his grandfather
and was sad the old man
could not return his gesture.

Cecil Rajendra

Grandfather's Holiday

Blue sky, paddy fields, grandchild's play,
Deep ponds, diving stage, child's holiday;
Tree shade, barn corners, catch-me-if-you-dare,
Undergrowth, *parul*-bushes, life without care.
Green paddy, all a-quiver, hopeful as a child,   5
Child prancing, river dancing, waves running wild.

Bespectacled grandfather old man am I,
Trapped in my work like a spiderwebbed fly.
Your games are my games, my proxy holiday,
Your laugh the sweetest music I shall every play.   10
Your joy is mine, my mischief in your eyes,
Your delight the country where my freedom lies.

Autumn sailing in, now, steered by your play,
Bringing white *śiuli*-flowers to grace your holiday.
Pleasure of the chilly air tingling me at night,   15
Blown from Himālaya on the breeze of your delight.
Dawn in Āśvin, flower-forcing roseate sun,
Dressed in the colours of a grandchild's fun.

Flooding of my study with your leaps and your capers,
Work gone, books flying, avalanche of papers.   20
Arms round my neck, in my lap bounce thump—
Hurricane of freedom in my heart as you jump.
Who has taught you, how he does it, I shall never know—
You're the one who teaches me to let myself go.

Rabindranath Tagore
Translated by William Radice

Notes and activities

Hide And Seek *Vernon Scannell*

Questions to discuss

How does Scannell make the poem dramatic—as though the action is taking place now? How does he create a sense of urgency in line 11?

One might say that the poem is in two halves. Where does the change occur? What does this change reflect in the speaker of the poem?

Hide And Seek *Thom Gunn*

Questions to discuss

What activities are going on in the first 21 lines? What does 'whoosh' (line 10) suggest about the skateboarders? What do lines 26–30 suggest about the children? Is there a connection between these lines and lines 22–25? Does the word 'hugging' in the last line and the image of lines 31–35 suggest a connection between these lines and line 22–30?

Write a comparison of these two poems. You might begin by making notes about: the situation * of the poems; the details on which each poet concentrates to build up a picture of the scene; the dramatic qualities of the poems; the 'meaning' of the poems.*

Entering The City *Tony Connor*

'Denizen' (line 19): an inhabitant

Questions to discuss

What impression do you gain of the city? Find out what you can about Pericles, Athens, Caesar and Rome. What contrast is being made between those people and places and the modern city? What is the speaker's attitude to the city?

Dumb Insolence *Adrian Mitchell*

Questions to discuss

What impression do we get of the speaker? What impression does he have of the world? What phrases are repeated in the poem and what effect does the repetition have?

Either write a letter from the poem's speaker to a friend about his life or write an account, in prose, of a day in the boy's life, at home and at school—you might write the account as a diary entry in the first person.

Poem Of Distant Childhood   *Noémia da Sousa*

Questions to discuss
What impression do you gain of the poet's childhood and how is that impression created? What words and phrases are especially vivid? What contrasts are there between the poet's childhood and her present life? How are these contrasts suggested? How does she suggest that this change occurred? What images suggest the 'brotherhood' of the poet's childhood?

Poem For My Sister   *Liz Lochhead*

'Peever' is a game.

Questions to discuss
What does 'strut' (line 2) suggest about the little sister? What does 'peck' (line 11) suggest about her? What contrasts are there between the sisters? What does the poem suggest about their feelings for each other?

Think and, if possible, talk about the problems you have had in life and write a poem to a younger relative giving advice about growing up.

1945   *Geoffrey Summerfield*

'Auschwitz, Buchenwald, and Belsen' (line 7): concentration camps set up by the Nazis before and during the Second World War
'The Spanish Inquisition' (line 11): a very cruel tribunal in Spain in the sixteenth century, which had people tortured to try and establish their religious beliefs and change them, if necessary
'Genghis Khan' (line 12): a cruel and powerful political dictator in the late 12th and early 13th centuries

Questions to discuss
What comparisons are being made between past and present and adult and child in the poem? In what way is it significant that the lesson in stanza 5 is History? The names 'Puncher and Kicker and Belter' (line 24) are all parodies; of what names are they parodies and what is the point of the parody? What is the poet suggesting about childhood?

It is interesting to compare Summerfield's feelings about childhood with da Sousa's. What do the two writers feel about childhood? What are their intentions in writing their poems? With which of them do you feel more in sympathy?
The two poems are written in very different styles. Make notes on the differences you can see and hear. Do these differences reflect the different intentions of the poets?

Cowboy   *Richard Hill*
Questions to discuss
How can an afternoon be described as 'thirsty' (line 2)? What is the first detail that lets us know that the poem is really about children? What details in the poem are comic? What is our attitude to the game? What was the speaker's attitude to the game when he was a child?

Write a dramatic account of a childhood game, bearing in mind the last three poems, trying to build up a clear picture of the situation and of the feelings and sensations involved in playing.

My Papa's Waltz   *Theodore Roethke*
Questions to discuss
What impression do you gain of the family in the poem? What sort of people are the mother and father and how can we tell? How would you describe the relationship between the speaker and his father?

Write about the relationship between yourself and someone in your family— as poetry or prose.

Leave-Taking   *Cecil Rajendra*
'lachrymose': tearful
'inimitable': impossible to imitate

Write a comparison between this poem and Tagore's 'Grandfather's Holiday' which also looks at the relationship between a grandfather and his grandchild. Focus on how the poems are narrated, what their themes are, and on their forms and rhythms.

Grandfather's Holiday   *Rabindranath Tagore, translated by William Radice*
This poem was written in 1922 and hinges on the Bengali word 'chuti' for which there is no real equivalent in English. In ordinary spoken Bengali it means 'holiday' but it also suggests a state of mind in which there is no difference between work and play: a state of delight, of freedom (see Ted Hughes 'Work And Play' in *Poetry Horizons Volume 2.*
'proxy': someone who acts or votes for someone else
'roseate': like a rose

Ideas for Coursework Folders

You will find here not only ideas for your Literature coursework folder, but also for your folder or for classwork in English Language. You should, of course, check with your teacher what the particular requirements of your syllabus are before you start. There may be a word limit or a specific style in which you are asked to write. These ideas will be suitable for most syllabuses.

1 Selection of 6–10 poems by theme
Once you have selected poems based on a common theme (and the index on p139 will help you), you should concentrate your notes on the differences between the poems as well as on their similarities. You might mention mood, tone, intensity of feeling, degree of detail, form, and what you think the writer's intention is. You might be able to group them in various ways, and may wish to say which of the poems you have chosen (you don't have to limit yourself to the poems in this anthology) you think is the most successful. This could, if you wanted it to, become a longer piece of writing for your folder, and might link with the actual making of your own anthology.

2 Selection of poems by one poet
In *Poetry Horizons Volume 2* there is a section devoted to three poets: John Betjeman, Sylvia Plath and Langston Hughes. You may wish to put off writing about one poet until then. On the other hand, if there is a particular poet in this anthology that you enjoy (and there are several poems here by poets such as Edwin Morgan, Charles Causley and Vernon Scannell which might offer a starting point) you might like to find more of his or her poems and write about them. Ask your teacher and/or librarian for help.

3 Selection of poems by region or culture
There are poems in this anthology by writers from Scotland, Ireland, Wales, England, Australia, Singapore, the West Indies, the USA, Africa, India, Cuba, East Germany, China and Mozambique. You may wish to find more poems from one of these countries and to see if you can identify any common characteristics between them. Again, you could make your own anthology before your start this kind of writing.

4 Selection of poems by form
Another way to group poems is by their form (that is to say, by the way the words are arranged on the page; see *Glossary*). In this anthology you will probably find it easiest to take the poems in the 'Telling' section, as they are all 'narrative' poems of a sort. For example, you may wish to compare the way the stories are told in a selection of these poems. See the notes to 'Telling'.

5   Writing about one poem

The 'key' poems in this anthology are provided with full notes to help you gain a richer response to them. You may wish to take one of them and write about it in one of various ways: (a) you could write a personal account of how you have come to a fuller understanding of the poem after several readings (b) you could write a more formal analysis of the poem or (c) you could give reasons as to why you prefer it to other poems in the anthology.

Of course, you could choose *any* poem to write about, as long as there is enough to write about it. To ensure you have enough to write, you should choose a poem of some substance.

6   Comparing two or three poems

Taking two or three poems to compare is probably easier than writing about just one poem, because you will be able to note the similarities and differences between the poems. You could take poems in any of the four categories mentioned in 1–4 above, or select two or three poems that have less in common. Some poems suitable for comparison immediately spring to mind: the poems entitled 'Digging' by Edward Thomas and Seamus Heaney (in *Observing*) and 'Hide and Seek' by Thom Gunn and Vernon Scannell (in *Childhood*), but there are many other possibilities.

7   Comparing poetry with prose

'Prose' is ordinary spoken and written language in a direct, straightforward arrangement, as opposed to poetry where there is a conscious rhythmic arrangement of words to convey a feeling or idea. Stories, novels, letters and these notes are written in prose. Prose only breaks into lines because the edge of the page won't allow it to go any further.

There are at least two possible ways in which you can compare poetry with prose: (a) you could take one of the poems in the anthology and re-write it as if it were prose, then make notes as to what is lost by this 'translation' or (b) you could find a passage of prose—or write one yourself for that matter!—on the same theme as one of the poems, and then compare the two pieces of writing.

If you want a piece of prose for your English folder, you could write an 'answer' to one of the poems here, or write on a similar theme. It may be possible for you to include some poetry in your English folder too, but you should check with your teacher before you attempt this.

8   Presenting a selection of poems

Which poems in this anthology would you select if you had to introduce poetry to a new reader? You would want to provide a wide range of types, and could write an interlinking text to help introduce them. This piece of work need not confine itself to your coursework folder, but could form the basis of a live or recorded talk.

9   Recorded discussion

Take any of the approaches suggested above, and rather than aim towards a written account, use the approach as the basis for a taped discussion with a small group of fellow-students. You may then wish to write down the discussion, and edit it for inclusion in your folder. This will be an interesting exercise in itself, and will teach you a great deal about how people discuss and something of the relationship between speech and writing.

10   Reading the poems aloud

You may like to try reading one of the poems in at least two ways, shedding a different light on the poem with each reading. Having recorded the readings, you could write a piece comparing their qualities and the aspects of the poem they emphasise.

Glossary

Alliteration: the repetition of the same initial sound in words close together; 'pennies and pounds' or 'the golden goose' are both examples of alliteration. Alliteration is often used in advertisements for much the same purpose that it is used in poetry.

Assonance: similar, but not identical, vowel sounds. Identical vowel sounds create *rhyme*; for example, 'good' and 'should' rhyme; 'shook' and 'should' do not rhyme but the similar vowel sound between them is an example of assonance.

Ballad: ballads would originally have been sung or recited. They were once a very popular form of entertainment and one of the characteristics of ballads is that they tell stories. Ballads nearly always have a very regular rhythm* and rhyme scheme.

Dramatic monologue: a poem written as though it is being spoken by one person, usually to another who does not speak. The speaker, while talking of other things, reveals a great deal about his or her character.

Form: the shape and structure of a poem; the way the words are arranged on the page. In many poems there is a regular form; the poet may have used four line stanzas* consisting of ten syllables per line, for instance. Rhyme may play a part in determining the form of a poem: a poem may be written in lines that rhyme in pairs. A poem may well not have a regular form; in other words, the form can be irregular.

Image: a picture in words; a phrase which is meant to make one visualise or experience what is being described.

Metaphor: a comparison not introduced by 'like' or 'as'; for example, 'he was a stubborn mule in the argument' is a metaphor whereas 'he argued like a stubborn mule' is a simile.* Note that neither the simile nor the metaphor suggest that 'he' had any mulish qualities (such as four legs) apart from a mule's stubbornness and, possibly, stupidity.

Narrative: a story; the telling of a story, which usually involves characters engaged in doing something.

Persona: the narrator or speaker of a poem; that part of one's character that one chooses to present to the rest of the world. You would assume a different persona when speaking to your head teacher from the one you might assume when speaking to a child younger than you.

Personification: giving human characteristics, such as speech or personality, to animals, objects or ideas.

Rhythm: all words, when spoken, have a rhythm; that is, a number of stressed syllables and a number of unstressed syllables, for one cannot avoid stressing some of the syllables one says. The stressed syllables create a rhythm. In poetry, as in music, the rhythm is often regular in which case one can call it 'metre' which means a regular rhythm.

Setting: the background against which the main action of a poem takes place. The setting may be (a) geographical—where the poem is set (b) the time—of day, of year or even the year itself—the poem is set (c) the social world from which the poem's speaker or characters come or (d) any combination of these three.

Simile: a comparison introduced by 'like' or 'as'. See metaphor.*

Situation: the situation of a poem refers to the speakers and/or characters in the poem (who is speaking to whom, for example); the relationship, if any between them and the position that they are in. The situation in 'Late Night Walk Down Terry Street', for example, is that the speaker is walking down a particular street late at night and is recording what he sees and hears.

Stanza: a division, usually regular, of a poem.

Subject: what the poem is about on the surface, as opposed to what it is really about, which is called 'theme'. For example, the subject of 'The Grey Squirrel' is a squirrel but for the theme of that poem, see below.

Syllable: a syllable is one single sound. 'Dog' has one syllable; 'rabbit' has two ('rab' and 'bit'); porcupine has three ('por', 'cu' and 'pine').

Theme: the main idea expressed by a poem or the main idea with which the poem is concerned. For instance, the theme of Humbert Wolfe's 'The Grey Squirrel' has to do with man's hypocrisy—pretending to be Christian when he is not.

Tone: it is easiest to determine tone by reading the poem aloud. Just as any phrase—'How are you?' for example—could be spoken in several very different tones of voice (and thus imply several very different emotions), so one must read a poem carefully to determine its tone. Remember that the tone might change during the course of the poem.

Suggested Cross-referencing by Theme

One of the suggestions for coursework in several GSCE syllabuses is that you could take 6–10 poems on a similar theme and compare the way the different poems handle that theme. Here is a guide to themes that occur in this selection, though of course you can find your own themes and further poems to discuss. *Childhood* is not mentioned here as it has a section to itself in the book.

Violence
'Glasgow 5 March 1971'   10
'An Attitude of Mind'   40
'Atomic Bomb'   75
'The Death Of The Ball Turret Gunner'   74
'O What Is That Sound'   76
'Does It Matter'   93
'Inspection'   100

The City
Edwin Morgan's poems in the *Observing* section   10, 11, 16
'Late Nght Walk Down Terry Street'   26
'September in Great Yarmouth'   99
'Dedicatory Poem'   21
'Entering The City'   120

People
'In The Snack Bar'   16
'The French Master'   14
'The Artist'   15
'White Child Meets Black Man'   47
'Her Dancing Days'   54
'Disillusion'   55
'Friedrich'   56
'Ballad Of Charlotte Dymond'   60
'Uncle Edward's Affliction'   80
'Warning'   98
'Hay For The Horses'   94
'The Building Site'   92

Index of Poets

Acknowledgements

The editors and publishers wish to thank the following for permission to reproduce poems:

Allison & Busby Ltd for 'Dumb Insolence' by Adrian Mitchell from *Nothingmas Day* and 'Hide And Seek' by Vernon Scannell; Andre Deutsch Ltd for '1945' by Geoffrey Summerfield from *Welcome*; Angus & Robertson (Aust) Ltd for 'In the Huon Valley' by James McAuley from *Collected Poems 1936–70*; Anthony Sheil Associates Ltd for 'The French Master' and 'Emperors of the Island' by Dannie Abse from *Golders Green*; Anvil Press Poetry for 'Fable' by Janos Pilinszky/Ted Hughes) from the *Oxford Book of Poetry*; Edward Arnold for 'Misfortunes Never Come Singly' by Harry Graham; Australian National University Press for 'The Pigs' by Geoffrey Lehman from *The Ilex Tree*; Bogle L'Ouverture Ltd for 'Leave Taking' by Cecil Rajendra from *Hour of the Assassin*; Jonathan Cape Ltd for 'The Castaways or Vote for Caliban' by Adrian Mitchell from *The Apeman Cometh*, 'Science, Where Are You?' and 'Catching Up On Sleep' by Roger McGough from *In the Glassroom*; Carcanet Press Ltd for 'Glasgow 5 March 1971' ('With A Ragged Diamond'), 'Glasgow 5 March 1971' ('Quickly the magistrate'), 'Chicago May 1971', 'In The Snack Bar', 'The Apple's Song' by Edwin Morgan from *Poems of Thirty Years* (1982); John Cassidy for 'An Attitude Of Mind' from *Poetry Introductions 3* published by Faber & Faber (1975); Chatto & Windus Ltd for 'Praise Of A Collie' by Norman MacCaig from *Trees of Strings*; Collins Publishers for 'Sergeant Brown's Parrot' by Kit Wright from *Rabbiting On*; Tony Connor for 'Entering the City'; Dodd Mead & Co Inc for 'We Wear The Mask' by Paul Laurence Dunbar from *The Complete Poems of Paul Laurence Dunbar*; Faber & Faber Ltd for 'A March Calf' by Ted Hughes from *Season Songs*, 'Dedicatory Poem' and 'Digging' by Seamus Heaney from *Wintering Out*; 'The Death of the Ball Turret Gunner' by Randall Jarrell from *The Complete Poems of Randall*, 'The River-Merchant's Wife: A Letter' by Li Po/Ezra Pound from *Collected Poems by Ezra Pound*, 'Hide And Seek' by Thom Gunn from *Passages of Joy*, 'My Papa's Waltz' by Theodore Roethke from *The Collected Poems of Theodore Roethke*, 'As I Walked Out One Evening' by W. H. Auden from *Collected Poems of W. H. Auden*, 'Sunday Morning Among The Houses Of Terry Street' from *Terry Street* by Douglas Dunn; Victor Gollancz Ltd for 'The World's A Minefield' by Iain Crichton Smith from *Love Poems and Elegies*; Michael Hamburger for 'Differences' by Günter Kunert from *East German Poetry*; Heinemann Educational Ltd for 'In Praise Of A Young Man' and 'To A Young Lady' from *Igbo Traditional Verse* (trans. Romanus Egudaa and Donatus Nwoga); Adrian Henri for 'Tonight At Noon' by permission of Deborah Rogers Literary Agents Ltd; David Higham Associates for 'Nursery Rhyme Of Innocence And Experience' and 'Friedrich' by Charles Causley from *Secret Destinations (Collected Poems)* published by Macmillan, 'Lord Sycamore', 'Ballad Of The Bread Man', 'The Ballad Of Charlotte Dymond' from *Collected Poems of Charles Causley* published by Macmillan; Richard Hill for 'Cowboy' from *Strictly Private* (ed. Roger McGough) published by Viking Kestrel; Olwyn Hughes for 'Metaphors' by Sylvia Plath from *Collected Poems* published by Faber & Faber; Jenny Joseph for 'Warning' from *Rose In The Afternoon*, published by J. M. Dent & Sons Ltd, 1974; Derek Mahon for 'September In Great Yarmouth' by permission of Oxford University Press from *Poems 1962–1978*; Macmillan Ltd for 'Breakfast' by W. W. Gibson from *Collected Poems 1905–25*; Martin Brian & O'Keeffe Ltd for 'Tinker's Wife' by Patrick Kavanagh from *The Collected Poems of Patrick Kavanagh*; Robert Marquez for 'Atomic Bomb' by Nicholas Guillen reprinted by permission of Monthly Review Foundation; Methuen Publishers for 'The Grey Squirrel' by Humbert Wolfe and 'On Certain Survivors' by Bertolt Brecht from *Poems 1913–56*; New Beacon Books for 'White Child Meets Black Man' by James Berry from *Fractured Circles*; Gareth Owen for 'The Building Site' from Salford Road; Oxford University Press (India) for 'Night of the Scorpion' by Nissim Ezekiel from *Latter Day Psalms*; Penguin Ltd for 'Grandfather's Holiday' from *Selected Poems* (trans. William Radice); Polygon Ltd for 'Poem For My Sister' by Liz Lochhead from *Dreaming Frankenstein and Collected Poems*; Presence Africaine for 'Poem Of Distant Childhood' by Noemia de Sousa from *Penguin Book of Women Poets*; Robson Books for 'Uncle Edward's Affliction'; George Sassoon for 'Does It Matter?' and 'They' by Siegfried Sassoon; Secker & Warburg Ltd for 'Camping Provençal' by Peter Reading; Stevie Smith for 'The River God' and 'The Jungle Husband' from *Collected Poems of Stevie Smith* (Penguin Modern Classics); Gary Snyder for 'Hay For The Horses' and 'Thin Ice' from *A Range of Poem*, Fulcrum 1966; Edward Thomas for 'Digging' by permission of Faber & Faber and Myfanwy Thomas from *Collected Poems of Edward Thomas*; University of Chicago Press for 'What Kind Of Guy Was He!' by Howard Nemerov from *Collected Poems of Howard Nemerov*, Virago Press Ltd for 'Her Dancing Days' by Anna Adams and 'Disillusion' by Maureen Burge from *Bread and Roses*; William Carlos Williams for 'The Artist'.

Whilst every effort has been made to contact the copyright-holders, this has not proved to be possible in every case.